THE ZEN MONASTERY COOKBOOK

STORIES AND RECIPES FROM A ZEN KITCHEN

COMPILED BY THE MONKS AT
THE ZEN MONASTERY PRACTICE CENTER
UNDER THE GUIDANCE OF CHERI HUBER

Cover design by Mary Denkinger
Cover art by Alex Mill

THE ILLUSTRATIONS IN THIS COOKBOOK were drawn by the monks-in-residence at the Zen Monastery Practice Center.

Monks contributing to this cookbook are as follows:

Dave
Faith
Melinda
Alex
Ann
Caverly
Josie
John
Rich
Jen
Kea
Deb
Shonen
Nadine
Phil

We offer this book in lovingkindness
to all the creatures who will benefit
from any effort we make
toward harmless living.

The following, from Zen Patriarch Dogen, hangs in the kitchen at our Monastery:

The Zen Cook

If we are sincere when cooking,
even the coarsest food can help us to exhibit
the seed of Buddhahood.

A Chief Cook must love water and rice
in the same way parents love their children.

Once the food has been prepared,
it must be cared for in the same way
we care for our own eyesight.

Acknowledgments

Providing healthful, wholesome, tasty food has been a big part of Monastery life from the beginning. Assisting people in the direction of non-violent cooking and eating is a natural continuation of the vow of harmlessness we take each day. The food has been very good.

When Dave McKay came to the Monastery and was given the job of Cook, the food took a quantum leap in excellence. His attention to detail, his commitment to service, his love of food, and his natural abilities as a cook expanded and refined what was already a great menu. Response to the meals went from compliments to raves.

We have been asked to produce a cookbook for years now. The project took form and direction when Dave turned his attention to it. Our thanks to Dave for bringing this cookbook together.

Christa Rypins, an inspired vegetarian cook, while assisting with the proofing of recipes, suggested that if we could put the same "heart" in the cookbook that people sense in the food at the Monastery, the cookbook, too, would go from good to great. We thank Christa for suggesting the introductions to the sections and the stories and drawings from the monks.

Then, as always, we handed a big stack of disks, papers, and drawings to June Shiver, who, once again (as she has done with our ten previous books), sat at the computer, hour after hour, turning a disorderly pile into the book you have in your hands. Our deep gratitude to her for this.

Thank you to Arlene Mueller for her expert proofreading skills. Because of her generosity, this is a better book.

We wish to express our appreciation of and gratitude for everyone who, through the years, has lent a hand in the Monastery kitchen, helping to feed monks and retreatants, supporting monastic life, and deepening their own awareness and practice. We hope you find yourself in these pages.

These acknowledgments are not complete without an expression of the love and gratitude we feel toward Cheri, our Guide. Whether it is burning the midnight oil to make this cookbook a reality, steadfastly guiding us to reveal our long held habits of suffering, or prodding us back on course when we've wandered off, she is willing to do whatever is necessary to allow us to discover for ourselves the compassion and willingness that is our True Nature. It is her vision, guidance and unlimited devotion to the practice of compassionate awareness that has inspired, motivated, and unerringly directed us along the road to freedom.

Preface

This cookbook is a reflection of the spiritual practice of those who were assigned Monastery Cook. It is the product of half a dozen years' labor. The recipes originate from a variety of sources, including the marvelous The Peaceful Palate, by Jennifer Raymond, and other fine cookbooks (see References). Especially, they originate from the creativity of the Monastery cooks who find a recipe, or make one up, and adapt it to the nutritional guidelines of the Monastery.

At the Zen Monastery Practice Center we offer a "privileged environment" which springs from and is nourished by compassion for all beings--two-footed, four-footed, multi-footed; walkers, crawlers, hoppers, slitherers, and fliers. The food we serve is an integral part of the privileged environment. Recipes are carefully selected and ingredients are chosen for nutritional value. When possible, we harvest vegetables from our organic gardens and serve them the same day. The food is simple, wholesome, and without any of the extra fats, sugars and additives commercially prepared foods rely on. It tastes like itself, which for many people is a new and wonderful experience.

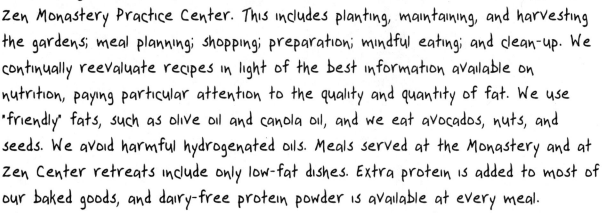

Every aspect of the daily schedule is part of the training in spiritual practice offered at the Zen Monastery Practice Center. This includes planting, maintaining, and harvesting the gardens; meal planning; shopping; preparation; mindful eating; and clean-up. We continually reevaluate recipes in light of the best information available on nutrition, paying particular attention to the quality and quantity of fat. We use "friendly" fats, such as olive oil and canola oil, and we eat avocados, nuts, and seeds. We avoid harmful hydrogenated oils. Meals served at the Monastery and at Zen Center retreats include only low-fat dishes. Extra protein is added to most of our baked goods, and dairy-free protein powder is available at every meal.

To encourage "one less act of violence" (from an essay by Cheri Huber by that title), we serve vegetarian fare that includes some eggs and dairy. This fare may be "easier to swallow" for those new to the idea of a meatless diet. The final step on the path from a meat-based diet to a vegetarian diet is a big one. We offer these "lacto-ovo" recipes as stepping stones along that path. Also, vegan dishes are served at most meals to accommodate diets that include no animal products.

Because our society considers eating "meat" the only "normal" way to eat, many Monastery visitors have their first encounter with strictly vegetarian fare while here with us. We hope they leave with a new understanding and appreciation of foods not acquired by killing other creatures, and we hope they will add more vegetarian choices to their diets.

This cookbook would not exist if it weren't for the many retreat participants who raved about the meals they ate and asked (begged, pleaded) for copies of recipes. They formed a chorus over the years of "WHEN WILL THE COOKBOOK BE READY?"

The cookbook is ready, and we offer it in lovingkindness.

Table of Contents

Dedication

The Zen Cook

Acknowledgments

Preface

How To   1

Tips and Suggestions   11

Soups   14

Asparagus   17

Green Velvet   18

Potato-Leek   19

Cream of Cauliflower   20

Cream of Celery   21

Cream of Spinach   22

Cream of Tomato   23

Corn and Baby Lima Bean Chowder   24

Winter Squash   25

Yellow Split Pea-Squash   26

Yellow Split Pea-Vegetable   27

Split Pea   28

Red Lentil and Squash   29

Black Bean   30

Minestrone   31

Miso-Onion   32

Summer Fruit   33

Vichyssoise   34

A Once in a Lifetime Experience   36

It's How, Not What   38

The Pupil and the Black Pot   40

Salads   42

Super Salad with Broccoli, Walnuts, and Feta   45

Raw Carrot Beet Salad   46

Curried Spinach   47

Tomato and Avocado   49

Waldorf   50

Fruit   53

Cucumber   55

Basic Coleslaw   56

Fruity Carrot   57

Black Beans and Corn   58

Nutty Rice   59

Nutty Rice Salad Dressing   60

Simple Fat-Free Dressing   61

Lemon-Thyme Dressing   62

The First Thing that Happens   63

This Will Never Work   65

Because That's What You've Been Practicing   67

Breads   69

Biscuits (aka: Cat Heads)   72

Sweet Potato Biscuits   73

Corn Bread   74

Basic Muffins   75

Bran Muffins   76

Orange Pecan Muffins   77

Maple Buttermilk Muffins   78

Brown Bread   79

Apricot Bread   80

Carrot Bread   81

Pancakes   82

French Toast   83

Bread Therapy   84

Bread of Life   86

Drop Biscuits   87

Basic Yeast Bread Recipe   88

Bread Sequence at a Glance   92

Yeast Bread Variations   92

Cinnamon Buns   94

Let the Ingredients Do the Talking   96

Main Dishes   97

Tofu Pot Pie with Dumplings   99

Spaghetti Sauce   101

Meatballs   102

Chunky Tomato Sauce   103

Bountiful Lasagna   104

Manicotti or Stuffed Shells   105

Tofu Manicotti or Stuffed Shells   106

Pasta with Creamy Tofu   107

Enchilada Casserole   108

Black Bean and Spinach Burritos   110

Chilaquiles Casserole   112

Mjeddrah   113

Curried Mushrooms and Chickpeas   114

Yellow Dal   115

Rajma (Curried Red Kidney Beans)   116

Vegetable and Tofu Stir-Fry   117

Orange Stir-Fry Sauce   119

Fried Rice   120

Marinated Tofu   121

Five Varieties of Baked Tofu   122

Tofu Stew   125

Tofu Burgers   126

Tofu Croquettes   127

Tofu Loaf   128

Tofu with Tartar Sauce   129

Chili Beans   131

Corn Pone   132

Soysage   133

Phil's Dish   134

Hash   135

Black-Eyed Peas   136

Macaroni and Cheese   137

Cheri's Pizza   138

Pizza   139

The Blind Monk and the Carrots   141

Lines from the Kitchen   142

Tofu Dave   144

Nothing to Do with Cooking   146

Side Dishes

Side Dishes   148

Tuscan Beans   149

Refried Beans   150

Oven Roasted Beets   151

Scrambled Tofu-Potato   152

Mashed Potatoes   153

Gravy   154

Scalloped Potatoes   156

Mushrooms Sautéed in Broth   157

Yams with Cranberries and Apples   158

Applesauce   159

Apricot Chutney   160

Spiced Tomato Chutney   161

Oven Fries   162

Practice Like Your Shirt Is On Fire   163

Hungry Ghosts   164

About Rice, Sort Of   165

Spreads

Spreads   167

The Original Tofu Spread   168

Mock Tuna Salad   169

Hummus   170

Tofu Hummus   171

Tofu (Egg) Salad   172
Tofu-Mushroom Spread   173
Tofu-Spinach Spread   174
Tofu-Artichoke Spread   175
Tofu-Avocado Spread   176
Miso Walnut Spread   176
Tofu-Basil Spread   177
Tofu-Ginger-Sesame Spread   178
Tofu-Horseradish-Olive Spread   178
Tofu-Miso Spread   179
Tofu-Zucchini-Sunflower Spread   180
White Bean Spread   180

Open-Faced Breadless Fall Sandwich   181
Yummiest Cake Ever   182
The Science Project   183
Designer Carafes   184

Desserts

Desserts   185
Baked Pears   187
Baked Apples   188
Chinese Chews   189
Chocolate Chip Cookies   190
Monk's Favorite Chocolate Cookies   191
Carmel Cookies   192
Ghirardelli Brownies   193
Chocolate Tofu Pudding   194
Rhubarb-Strawberry Pudding   195
Graham Cracker Crusts   196
Crumb Topping   197
Apple-Berry Crisp   198
Tofu Chocolate Pie   199
Lemon Meringue Pie   200
Cherry Pie   201
Pumpkin Pie   202
Chocolate Cake   203

A Glorious Child-Like Experience 204

Carrot Cake 205

Raw Apple Cake 206

Gingerbread 207

Lemon Sauce 208

Walnut Crumb Cake 209

Chocolate Pudding Cake 211

Italian Cheesecake 212

Strawberry Sauce 213

Tofu Cheesecake 214

Cheesecake 216

Chocolate Frosting 217

Tofu Chocolate Icing 218

The Icing on the Cake 219

The Whole Shopping List Is About Me 220

Odds and Ends 221

Granola 222

Prune Purée 224

Soymilk 225

Soymilk Saga 229

In the Beginning 231

The Fundamentals 235

For the Record 237

Mindful Eating 243

References 244

How To

We thought we would put together some basic cooking information for folks who are new to vegetarian cooking, and for those times when you just can't remember how long to steam a beet or how much water to use when cooking polenta. We hope the following will help you to get started.

Cooking without Oils or Butter

The biggest part of low fat cooking is learning how to do without oils and butter. This may seem a daunting proposition at first. In fact, it is easy to do. Oils and butter serve three primary functions in traditional cooking: to prevent food from sticking to skillets and pans; to provide rich and/or flaky textures to baked goods such as cakes, breads, and piecrusts; and to serve as a base to carry the seasoning through the dish that is being prepared. Maybe we should take a look at each of these in turn.

The first is simple to compensate for. We use a fat-free cooking spray to grease baking pans and casserole dishes, and this does the job very well. There are several varieties on the market, and they are easy to find. Another option is to use a "mister," a device that imitates cooking sprays without the waste of an empty can. You add a little oil, pump a few times to pressurize the canister, and the mister will produce a very fine spray, enough to coat the pan without any excess. We have not had good luck with these so far, but that may be because of the large volume of cooking we do. If you know of something that works, we'd love to hear about it.

When cooking food in a skillet over a burner, we use a technique we call the "steam sauté." It's a matter of using small amounts of water, instead of oil, to keep food from sticking. To steam sauté, heat up the skillet, add a couple of tablespoons of water and whatever you are cooking, and continue to add water bit by bit as needed until done. Whenever things dry out and start to stick, that's when you add more water. You'll notice that you will be required to stir more often than you normally would, and that you'll need to keep an eye on things a little more carefully. Your food will cook very satisfactorily this way. It will not

1

produce the browning effect of frying. For example, you could cook tofu all day this way and it will never brown, but this is usually not much of an inconvenience.

You will need to substitute something for the oil or butter in cake and bread recipes so that the consistency of the batter or dough will be correct, and so that the result will have a nice, moist texture. All sorts of things will work: applesauce, mashed sweet potato, yams, winter squash, puréed prunes (see the prune puree recipe, page 224). Just substitute one of these in equal amounts for the oil or butter. It doesn't matter which, although you may want to keep in mind that each will add some of its flavor to what you are baking. It can be argued that prune purée works the best of all of these, but we generally keep a jar of unsweetened applesauce in the refrigerator to use for this purpose because that's the simplest

 solution for us and because it has the most neutral flavor. Now, the breads and cakes that will be produced after this substitution will be slightly different from what you are used to. They will be denser, and they will not be "short" (a cookie that snaps crisply in half is called "short"). Alas, we have tried and tried to create a traditional piecrust recipe (flour, butter, salt, and water) that works without

the fat and have failed utterly. Many people, however, find that they do not miss the oil or butter at all, and, in fact, enjoy things that are baked this way even more because they are "clean" and feel good in your belly. We have compromised in this book where it was necessary (a biscuit without oil, for example, is a cracker), but that is not too often.

We find that, without the oil, we need to go a little heavier on the seasonings. Fat enhances the flavor of things. We also tend to turn towards dishes that are full of flavor by themselves because of the delicious foods that constitute them and away from those that rely heavily on the oil or butter to be effective. There is no reason to put oil in a soup made from a nice bean broth, for example (see the introduction to the soups section) because it is so tasty all by itself.

Substituting for Eggs and Dairy Products

If you want to reduce or eliminate eggs and/or dairy products from your diet, this is an easy thing to do, and it is not necessary to go without the foods that you are used to eating. Most recipes can be adapted to accommodate a vegan diet. Soymilk, for example, may be substituted for cow's milk pretty much across the board. If you are fortunate, as we are, to have thick, unsweetened, homemade soymilk to use, the food you will turn out will be just as good or better than food made with cow's milk. The texture of baked goods such as biscuits or cornbread will be slightly different but no less appealing. Finding something to exchange for cheese, cottage cheese, and sour cream is more difficult. There are some satisfactory non-dairy cheeses on the market that will do, and in many cases mashed tofu will work fairly well, but what you will produce with these substitutions will not be exactly what you are used to. Some people really like how dishes turn out when made this way, and some don't, so you'll have to experiment and see what you like. The more a dish relies on the cheese or sour cream, the more it will be altered by the substitutions. Occasionally, you may find something that does just as well or better without the dairy, such as Tofu Manicotti (page 106). And occasionally you will find something that does not work at all, and then you'll have that experience.

In most cases an "egg replacer" (a starchy powder sold under a variety of brand names at natural food stores) will do fine as a substitution for real eggs. The effect will not be quite the same--for example, your cake will not set up quite so well--but the difference will be minimal. Egg replacers, in our experience, will not work to make a custard or something similar (such as French toast, or rice pudding), and they cannot be made into a meringue (as in lemon meringue pie), but they do fine as part of a muffin or cookie.

Cooking Grains

Most people in North America eat only two grains--wheat, in the form of bread and pasta, and rice--but there are many other choices available. If you are unaware of all that is out there, just trot down to your natural foods store and check it out. The varieties of rice alone that you can find these days is marvelous. We enjoy pasta and rice as well as the next gang of monks, but we're also partial to spelt, which makes excellent bread and can be eaten as a cooked cereal; to quinoa, a wonderful grain from South America with a nutty flavor; to bulgur wheat, a dark brown grain that is especially good with creamy things and cheese; and to millet, a grain which has supported the ancient cultures of the East for eons. We also enjoy couscous, which is a type of pasta (made from wheat) from the Middle East.

The method for cooking most grains is the same: measure some water, some grain, and some salt into a pot that has a tight-fitting lid (see the chart below for quantities); bring it all to a boil, cover, and lower the heat to the lowest possible setting; wait, and your rice or quinoa will be done when all the water has been absorbed. It's best not to peek while the pot is simmering, as this will allow some of the steam to escape. The following chart will also give you approximate cooking times:

GRAIN	RATIO: WATER/GRAIN	COOKING TIME
white rice, any type	1 1/2:1	15-20 minutes
brown rice, any type	2:1	35-40 minutes
wild rice	4:1	1 hour, or more
millet	2:1	15-20 minutes
quinoa	2:1	20 minutes
bulgur wheat	2:1	15-20 minutes
couscous	1 1/4:1	5 minutes
polenta	3:1	10 minutes

Polenta is coarsely ground cornmeal, a staple in parts of Italy. If you are from the Southeast, you will notice that what people are talking about when they use the word "polenta" is actually grits, but people won't eat it if you call it that. To cook polenta, boil the water and pour the cornmeal into the pot in a slow stream, stirring as you go to prevent it from clumping. Lower the heat and continue to stir for ten minutes (or less), until the meal has swelled and absorbed all the liquid.

We figure a cup of any of these grains, uncooked, will serve three people. A pinch of salt is usually appreciated.

Cooking Dry Beans and Other Legumes

Beans have the reputation of being troublesome to cook, but this is not our experience at all. They need a little time, it's true, but not much attention, and the pleasure of having a pot of pintos or black-eyed peas simmering cheerfully on the stove while you tend to other things would pay for twice the effort.

The first step is to sort your beans. Often they come in from the field with tiny stones or clods of dirt, and these will sometimes survive the cleaning process that happens before they arrive on your supermarket shelves. Of course, these will need to be removed. We like to spread the beans out on a cookie sheet to sort them so we can see more clearly. Beans will cook best if they are soaked for at least four hours before they are cooked. We like to soak them over night and cook them in the morning. If you are short on time, an alternate way is to bring the beans and plenty of water to a boil, remove from heat and cover, and then soak them for only two hours before cooking. After the beans have been sorted and soaked, the next steps are to drain the soaking liquid, rinse, and put the beans in a pot, cover them with about two inches of fresh water, and bring it all to a boil. After the pot boils, reduce it to a quiet simmer, and cook the beans until they are soft enough to eat. The cooking time for most beans is the same, about an hour and a half. Large beans such as kidneys and pintos may take a little longer. Garbanzo beans (a.k.a. chickpeas) need to be cooked longer than most other legumes, usually two hours at least and often more. If you are cooking beans for a salad or a dish that requires them to hold their shape, you will want to begin checking them earlier. In addition, you will want to cook them as gently as possible. A lot of agitation in the water will cause many of the beans to burst. If you are not particular about the texture, as, for example, you would not be if you were making refried beans, then you can cook them for much longer provided they do not dry out. Black-eyed peas, crowder peas, and other field peas require less cooking time--forty-five minutes will usually do it. These do not need to be soaked necessarily, but it's still helpful. The same goes for split peas--unsoaked split peas will disintegrate after about an hour of cooking. Lentils and red lentils require only about thirty minutes.

Beans will take to just about any seasoning. Some herbs we like best with beans are basil, thyme, marjoram, dill, and celery seed; a mixture of chili powder and cumin is also a natural with beans (and a start in the direction of chili). We usually throw the seasonings in the pot for the last half-hour of cooking time, but we'll wait until they are cooked to add the salt, as salt seems to impede the cooking for some reason. Vegetables may be added towards the end to make a soup or a stew. Beans usually enjoy a little something sour, like vinegar or lemon juice, or even orange juice in the case of black beans.

Cooking with Tofu

Tofu has got to be the most wonderful thing to happen to vegetarian cooking since the vegetable. It is extremely high in protein and low in fat; it's easy to digest, unlike many other high protein foods; it is inexpensive and easy to produce; and best of all, it is almost completely neutral in flavor, shape, and texture and will adapt to an incredible range of ideas regarding its preparation. We eat it by the truckload at the Monastery. There are two types: Chinese style tofu, which is the sort that most people are familiar with, usually sold packed in water in plastic trays; and silken tofu, much richer than the other type, with a lovely satin texture, usually, but not always, sold in small vacuum-packed boxes. With the exception of a couple of desserts, all the tofu recipes in this book are written for the Chinese style. There are a number of tricks and techniques involving tofu to be aware of as you use this book.

--Pressing tofu: If a recipe asks that the tofu be "pressed," this means that it needs to have the excess water squeezed out of it without changing its shape, giving it a firmer and more substantial texture. To accomplish this, place the block of tofu between two cutting boards or two baking sheets, put a small weight on top (say, a 28 ounce can of tomatoes or a large glass of water), and leave it for thirty minutes or more. The more tofu you are pressing, the more weight you will need. During a recent retreat we pressed twenty pounds of tofu at one time and used a couple of huge flour buckets. We like to tilt our pressing contraption so that the water will drain right into the sink. If a recipe calls for the tofu to be "drained," you are not being asked to press it but simply to pour off the water it has been packed in.

--Marinating tofu: Tofu will eagerly accept any flavor you wish to give to it, and the most common way to do this is to use a marinade. Any liquid that has a flavor you enjoy will work as a marinade. You could simply use your favorite store-bought salad dressing or sauce, or you could make your own. For a very simple marinade, mix four teaspoons of soy sauce with a cup of water. This will make enough to marinate one pound of tofu and will add enough flavor that it can be baked and eaten like that. You could also add some garlic and ginger, rosemary, or some Dijon mustard. Instead of water you could add the soy sauce to orange or pineapple juice and marinate the tofu in that (this will make a nice addition to salads, especially if the tofu is baked for a little while first). Marinate tofu for at least two hours and preferably overnight, especially if the pieces are large.

--Baking tofu: the easiest way to prepare tofu is to bake it. Marinate the tofu first, then bake it one of two ways--at a high temperature (400°) in a pan for thirty to forty-five minutes, or at a very low temperature (250°) right on the oven racks for an hour or more. The two techniques will produce different results; you'll have to try each and see which you like best. There are several recipes in the Main Dish section for baked tofu, including a marinade that can be used as a sauce.

--Freezing tofu: One of the most interesting things you can do with tofu is to freeze it. The texture will radically change, making it tougher and more meat-like. Dishes that imitate the carnal fare that most of us were brought up on are often made with frozen tofu. It has been said that a farmer in Japan, after making a fresh batch of tofu, will sometimes set some of it outside under the eaves of his or her house to freeze in the night and thaw in the day until it is needed in the kitchen (don't worry--we don't do this with our tofu, but we enjoy the thought of it). You'll want your tofu to freeze solid, and then, when you're ready to use it, boil a pot of water and drop in the tofu to thaw. At this point, the excess water can be wrung out like a sponge, and the tofu is ready to use. See the Soysage and Sloppy Joe recipes in the Main Dish section for a couple of suggestions.

Steaming Vegetables

The easiest and simplest way to cook vegetables is to steam them. All you have to do is put half an inch of water in the bottom of a pot and bring it to a boil, add your veggies, cover the pot with a tight-fitting lid, and cook the food until done in the steam that builds inside the pot. You can refer to the chart below for approximate cooking times. It's a good idea not to peek into the pot, if you can help it, until there is a good chance that the food will be cooked. Peeking allows the steam to escape and interferes with the process. We like to use a "steaming basket," a contraption that you set in the bottom of the pot to raise the food out of the water. Without a basket, the bottom layer of broccoli or squash will boil rather than steam and, perhaps, be a little mushy. The time that is required to steam a vegetable depends on how big the pot is, how high the flame, and how cooked you like it, so the times listed below are approximations only.

Vegetable	Steaming Time	Vegetable	Steaming Time
broccoli	3-5 minutes	cauliflower	5-8 minutes
carrots	8-10 minutes	beet slices	20 minutes
summer squash	5-8 minutes	whole beets	25-30 minutes
diced potatoes	10 minutes	sliced sweet potatoes	10 minutes
whole potatoes	15-20 minutes	diced winter squash	10-15 minutes
green beans	5-8 minutes	greens	8-10 minutes
peas	5-7 minutes	peppers	3-5 minutes
artichokes	1 hour	fresh corn	7-10 minutes
onions	8-10 minutes	shredded cabbage	5-7 minutes

If you would like to serve two or more types of steamed vegetables at once, it will take a little math. For example, if you're cooking broccoli and carrots (a favorite combination of ours), steam the carrots for about five minutes, then add the broccoli. You will quickly learn to gauge more precisely how long to cook things to suit your taste and cooking equipment. Other combinations of vegetables we enjoy are cauliflower and peas, summer squash and corn, beets and greens (we usually steam these separately and serve the beets on top of the greens), and pretty much anything with peppers.

Roasting Vegetables

This is a wonderful way to cook vegetables, suited especially to root crops, but anything will work. The procedure is to cut your vegetables into large chunks, toss them with a tiny bit of olive oil and a pinch of salt and pepper, and roast them in an open pan in the oven at 450°. Try a mixture of carrots, beets, onions, and whole mushrooms--you can't beat it. A tablespoon or two of rosemary is a nice addition, as well. The time required to roast vegetables varies quite a bit depending on what type of vegetable it is, but you don't really have to worry about overcooking them, as they just get better and better the longer they roast. Around an hour will usually do it for root crops, less for other things. Try roasting carrots this way for a couple of hours. The process brings out their natural sweetness, and the result is better than candy.

Peeling Tomatoes

To peel a tomato, bring a large pot of water to a boil, core the tomato, and drop it in the water. Leave it there for a minute or so and then remove it from the water, rubbing off the skin with your fingers when it is cool enough to handle.

Baking winter squashes

The method used to bake winter squash is the same for all varieties, including pumpkin. First, cut the squash in half and scoop out the seeds; next, place the halves cut-side down in a baking dish and add a half-inch of water; finally, bake the squash in a pre-heated oven at 400° for about an hour. The time required depends upon the size and type of squash--when it is soft to the touch it is finished.

Thickening Liquids

One of the basic techniques in classic European cooking involves thickening liquids such as milk or stock to make a sauce, which would then be seasoned and served or used as a part of a larger dish. The traditional method of doing this requires an intimidating amount of fat, but this is not the only way. The same essential sauces can still be very tasty with little or no fat.

The basic idea is to mix the liquid (milk, soymilk, vegetable stock, bean stock, tomato juice) with a carefully measured thickener (flour, cornmeal, cornstarch), bring it to a simmer, and stir continuously while the thickener expands and absorbs some of the liquid, creating the sauce. Each thickener you might choose will produce a very different result. Flour will make a smooth and creamy sauce, for example, and for this reason we use it to make gravy and Pasta with Creamy Tofu. Cornstarch will make a silky textured sauce and is used a great deal in Oriental cooking and in desserts. The thickness of the sauce depends on the ratio between the liquid and the thickener. Use one to two tablespoons of flour per cup of water, or two to three teaspoons of cornstarch, depending on how thick you want the sauce to be. Two tablespoons of flour will yield a "medium" sauce. For a pudding, use three to four tablespoons of flour or one and a half to two tablespoons of cornstarch. You will notice that a couple of our recipes ask you to toast the flour before adding it to the liquid; this is done in order to compensate for the raw taste the flour will contribute to the sauce if it is not cooked thoroughly. When you make gravy, which is technically a "brown sauce" (as opposed to a "white sauce"), toast the flour thoroughly, and it will add to the color and flavor of the end product. To toast flour, heat a dry, thick-bottomed skillet over a medium flame, add the flour, and then stir it constantly with a flat-edged spatula or wooden spoon until it lightly browns. This takes a bit of practice. If you burn the flour, you'll have to start over as it will ruin the sauce. Cornstarch does not need to be toasted.

As you wander your way through this cookbook, you will find many instances when you will be required to use this technique, whether to thicken Cream of Asparagus Soup or prepare a stir-fry dish. In each case, you will be told specifically what to do, but always the thing to remember is to pay attention that you do not miss the critical moment when your sauce or pudding comes to a boil, and stir.

That's about all we can think of that you may need to know. Some of the introductions to the various sections of this book contain additional information along these lines (suggestions about how to cook soups or make a salad, for example). If you don't know how to do something, and you don't mind a little adventure, the best way to learn is to try and see what happens. That's the most fun way to learn, and, of course, this is what the whole thing is all about.

A Few Tips and Suggestions

Often people are impressed by the food we eat at the Monastery and by all the attention that goes into how it is provided, prepared, and served. Our diet represents a commitment to kindness towards ourselves, to the planet, and to the hearty enjoyment of what life makes available to us. Many times this is something people wish to take home with them to recreate in their own lives. This cookbook was written to assist those who have that wish. These recipes will serve as a practical starting place, we hope, for anyone who wants to develop self-awareness through the food they eat and to discover what is possible when consciousness is brought to the way we feed ourselves.

Here are a few suggestions of a general nature that we find helpful in creating a diet that nourishes body, mind, and spirit:

We encourage you to eat "clean" food. At the Monastery this means that we do not eat the flesh of other creatures. The closed-heartedness that is required to eat meat takes all the enjoyment out of the food, we feel, and sickens the spirit. Also, we find foods that please the senses but do not meet the needs of the body unsatisfying. If you feel bad after a meal, it may be a good idea (no matter how much you enjoyed the taste) to look at what you have eaten and what (what part of yourself) you have actually been feeding. We all decide for ourselves what food is "clean" and how we can eat that which will bring the most kindness and harmony into our lives. If you pay attention, the experience you have of yourself while you cook, eat, or grow or buy your food will assist you. The exploration of this issue requires a deep look into your relationship with yourself and your environment that will continue to benefit you for the rest of your life if you choose. Watch very carefully, and then remember to err well on the side of generosity. It's no fun at all to eat according to an idea of what is right. Look inside and eat according to the experience you find there of how you wish to live.

Provide for yourself the freshest and highest quality food you can find. You deserve it. Our society and the whole planet deserve it. The very best way to do this, of course, is to grow it yourself--there is nothing in the world so satisfying as

11

eating food from your own garden on the day it was harvested. Otherwise, check around for the market that has the best produce you can find. We would highly recommend that you buy organic food if you have a source for it. It can be a disheartening experience to spend time in the produce department of a large supermarket chain these days, knowing what has and has not gone into the food that you find there. Organic food tastes much better, has more of what your body needs, and is free of the toxins that remain in food that is "conventionally" grown. We are extremely fortunate in this respect. There is a large organic farm near the Monastery where we buy as much as possible of what we need to supplement what we grow in our garden.

The freshness of your food is also important. The produce in most large stores is often days old before it even appears on the shelf and has been trucked all over who knows where before it gets there. In many cases, the varieties of vegetables and fruits have been selected for their ability to absorb the impact of transportation rather than for flavor or nutritional value. Eat a store-bought tomato, and then eat one fresh out of somebody's garden--there's no comparison. You might see if there is a farmers market in your area or look for an independent produce stand. Often, in urban areas, it is not difficult to find small produce markets with food that is much higher quality than that found elsewhere (and way more fun to visit). When we go to Carmel, we shop at a tiny but packed stand managed by a Japanese family, and they always recognize us and greet us heartily, even though we're there only two days a year. We would also recommend that, once you have found the best possible source of fruits and vegetables, buy lots and lots of them and eat them all.

Get the kitchen equipment you feel you need. The frustration of trying to cook with inadequate gear can turn a person off cooking forever. You don't need much. Get stuff that works for you and get rid of anything that doesn't. Treat yourself to a cast iron soup pot; to a couple of nice saucepans; to some bread pans and a variety of other baking pans and casserole dishes; to a couple of sets of measuring cups and spoons; to a good knife and a cutting board; and, if you can afford it, to a blender or food processor. The pleasure you will receive from having the right stuff to cook your beautiful food in will negate the expense.

We suggest that you transform your kitchen into a place you love to be, if it is not already. Resist the temptation, if possible, to use your kitchen for purposes other than the preparation of food. If you have to slog through the piles of junk that you've left on your kitchen counter every time you want to cook, you won't cook much. At the Monastery the kitchen is as sacred a part of the whole as anyplace else. When we go to work in the kitchen, it is with the same intention that we take everywhere, that we might learn to be present to our lives and to the joy and contentment that is possible for us in each moment. Set aside the time to prepare food for yourself and commit yourself to being there, in that experience of yourself as you cook, as much as you are able to each time. Turn off the music and the television; turn your attention to your breath and to the experience of chopping the vegetables or stirring the soup. Make the time when you cook a special time that is just for you so that your heart is nourished by your efforts as much as your body is.

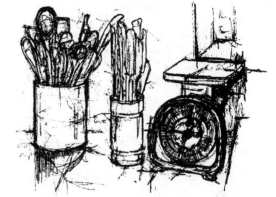

Above all else, have fun. As the Guide is fond of saying, "This is not a contest." If cooking is something you can fail at, you will not enjoy it, and your enthusiasm will not last long. Experiment, learn, and, if you do not take the results personally, everything will be part of the excitement.

Serve the food with the same care and respect that has gone into preparing it, taking care that it is as lovely to look at as it will be to eat. Use your best or favorite dishes every time, even if it's just for you. Eat the food you have prepared with great appreciation for all that has gone into it, and kiss the cook when you're finished.

Every part of the process--providing yourself with the food, preparing it, and eating it--is for you. It can be an expression of your love for yourself. Good luck, and let us know how it goes.

Soups

You'll find a great big pot of soup at the head of the table most evenings here at the Monastery. We work very hard, and it's a wonderful thing at the end of the day to ladle yourself a steaming bowlful, and then to slice yourself an inch-wide hunk of homemade bread to go with it. If you add on top of that some yummy spread and tomatoes and lettuce from the garden, it's easy to feel like you've been generously over-paid. Some of the best food that comes out of our kitchen is in the form of soups, many think, and the variety that is possible seems just about endless. We have red soups, green soups, yellow soups, black soups, orange soups, white soups, and even blue soups in the summer (see Summer Fruit Soup).

Soup making is actually very easy. The basic method goes like this: first, you decide what you want to put in your soup (vegetables, beans, and/or grains, generally) and get everything ready; then you cook it all up, add whatever sort of liquid you intend to use as a base and whatever seasonings you wish to try, simmer it all together for a few minutes to blend flavors, and, presto! If you are new to cooking soups you might want to practice for a bit with the recipes that follow and then branch out on your own and experiment in whatever direction pleases you. Pretty much anything goes. A lot of times our best soups are the ones that we throw together from the homeless odds and ends of things that have piled up in the refrigerator. Soups also do not generally depend upon oil or butter to be good, so it is an easy matter to convert just about any recipe you come across to a low or fat-free dish.

A word or two about the liquid "base" of your soups may be helpful. Traditionally a stock would be made by boiling the bones of some unfortunate creature to use as the soup's liquid, and the thought of making a soup without taking this step (or without using beef or chicken bouillon) is daunting to many beginning vegetarian cooks, but the truth is that this kindness opens up a whole world of better possibilities.

It is a very simple thing to make a vegetable stock, for example. Just save up the discarded scraps of whatever vegetables you've been eating lately (carrot peelings, onion and garlic skins, mushroom stems, etc), and then when you're ready to make your soup throw them all in a pot with some water and boil them for fifteen minutes, strain out the solids, and then use the liquid in the soup if you like how it tastes. The result of this process is often very delicious and will improve any soup, and additionally is loaded with the vitamins that were in the scraps that you used. Tomatoes are the most obvious thing to use to make a flavorful soup base. Canned or fresh tomatoes will both work: just cook them in water for about fifteen minutes, purée the tomatoes and water together to make a red broth, and then add whatever else you would like and continue simmering until it's all done.

Another excellent soup base is the water that is left over from cooking beans, especially kidney beans. For an easy soup, cook a handful of beans in plenty of water and add vegetables and seasonings for the last half-hour of cooking time. Split peas and red lentils make an especially excellent base because if you cook them long enough they will disentegrate into a thick (and very yummy) broth. Another possibility is to use winter squashes to make your soup base. Just bake the squash(s) (see the How-To section), pureé them in a blender or food processor, and then mix the pulp with however much water it takes to get the consistency you desire. If you want a soup that will impress people this is the way to go--some of our most popular soups are made this way.

We also enjoy using miso (a traditional Japanese seasoning, made from fermented soybeans usually) to make soups. There are many types of miso and they are all good as far as our experience goes. For the easiest of all possible soups, put a tablespoon of miso in a bowl and pour a cup of boiling water over it and mix it together. Root vegetables such as carrots, yams, and beets are especially good in miso soups.

It is also possible to make good cream soups without the fat that most recipes call for. These days we generally use homemade soymilk in our cream soups. To make a low-fat cream soup, cook whatever vegetables you would like in enough water to just cover them, then heat up some fat-free milk or soymilk (this is important--otherwise it will separate), and add it to the pot. Cream soups are often good puréed. Also, there is nothing wrong with using plain old water to make soup or with using vegetable bouillon to give it a little extra flavor.

You will learn how to use seasonings to enhance your soups with a little practice. A lot of times just a little salt and pepper will do it, especially if you've got vegetable stock or bean water to use as a base. You will notice as you go along what herbs and spices tend to be put together in things, and you will get a sense of how much is enough. This is the most fun part of soup making. You've got your soup all made, but it seems to need a little something, so you try a bit of this and then pinch of that, and then you find it--"Oh, the marjoram did it. How interesting." If you're experimenting, it's a good idea to start small and add a bit at a time rather than starting boldly and risking disaster, but that's a matter of style.

We hope you will enjoy the recipes that follow. They have comforted us through many a cold winter evening and have a special place in our hearts.

Asparagus Soup

We make this soup only once or twice a year, at the height of the asparagus harvest in the early spring, but we'd be happy to have it more if we could. Making the gravy is a little tricky but, if you are short on time or willingness, that step could be skipped--you would just get a thinner soup. In that event, you would heat up the milk and add it directly to the purée without the flour.

1 medium potato, peeled and cut into chunks
1 onion, chopped
1 1/2 pounds fresh asparagus, chopped
4 stalks celery, chopped
2 tsp. salt
1/8 tsp. pepper
1 Tbs. flour (white or whole wheat)
1 cup milk or soymilk

1. Sauté the onion in a bit of water until tender.
2. Add the potatoes, asparagus, celery, salt, pepper and enough water to just cover the vegetables, and bring it all to a boil. Simmer until everything is done.
3. Meanwhile, toast the flour in a dry skillet until lightly browned. Allow it to cool for a couple of minutes, then whisk it into the milk and gently bring it to a simmer, stirring constantly to prevent burning. This gravy will thicken as it comes to a boil; when it has, stir it into the soup. Add more water if needed.

Serves four to six.

Green Velvet Soup

This is one of the cook's favorites. For a special treat try adding a handful of ground almonds to step 3.

3/4 cup green split peas
1 onion, chopped
2 stalks celery, diced
4 cups zucchini, diced
1 bay leaf
1/4 tsp. basil
1/8 tsp. pepper
2 tsp. salt
1 pound spinach, washed and chopped
1/4 cup parsley, chopped

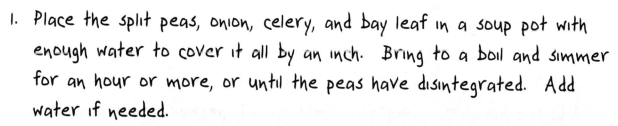

1. Place the split peas, onion, celery, and bay leaf in a soup pot with enough water to cover it all by an inch. Bring to a boil and simmer for an hour or more, or until the peas have disintegrated. Add water if needed.
2. Remove the bay leaf, then add the remaining ingredients, return to a simmer, and cook until the zucchini is tender (about five minutes).
3. Pureé everything in a blender, then return to the soup pot, add water as needed, and serve hot.

Serves six.

Potato-Leek Soup

We've been researching the origins of some of the old Monastery recipes so that we can give credit. All we know about this one is that it came to us via somebody named Joe. If you happen to be Joe-- thanks. We've enjoyed this soup for a lot of years.

4 pounds potatoes, chopped

3 leeks, whites and fresh part of greens, chopped

3 Tbs. parsley, chopped

6 garlic cloves

3 Tbs. fresh dill, chopped (or one tablespoon dried)

3 Tbs. fresh basil, chopped (or one tablespoon dried)

2 cubes vegetable bouillon

1 tsp. salt

3/8 tsp. (or less) pepper

pinch sugar (optional)

1. Cover potatoes with water and add a little salt. Boil until they are tender. Drain and reserve liquid. Mash all but one-fourth cup.

2. Dissolve bouillon in hot water. Add leeks, garlic, parsley, basil, and dill and sauté until tender. Add to mashed potatoes. Add enough of the reserved liquid in which the potatoes were cooked to make a soupy consistency. The soup will thicken as it stands, and more liquid may be added before serving.

3. Add salt and pepper and cook for about half hour. Adjust seasonings, adding sugar if necessary.

Serves eight to ten.

Cream of Cauliflower Soup

1 head cauliflower, in chunks

3 celery stalks, sliced

1 onion, chopped

3 medium-sized red potatoes, peeled and cut into chunks.

6 cloves garlic, minced

5 cups water

2 tsp. salt

1/8 tsp. white pepper

1/8 tsp. nutmeg

3 cups soymilk (unsweetened preferably)

1 pound frozen peas

1. Place the celery, potatoes, onions, garlic, salt, and water in a pot and bring to a boil. Cook for five minutes, then add the cauliflower and continue cooking until all the vegetables are tender.
2. Purée these ingredients in a food processor or blender until smooth.
3. Warm up the soy milk and add it along with the remaining ingredients. Heat thoroughly without boiling and serve.

Serves eight.

Cream of Celery Soup

2 medium-sized potatoes, peeled and diced
4 cups chopped celery
1 cup minced celery
3 cups water
1 1/4 tsp. salt
1 cup finely minced onion
1 tsp. celery seed
1 cup milk or soymilk, warmed*
a pinch of white pepper

1. Sauté the onion and chopped celery in a bit of water until very tender.
2. Add the water, potatoes, and all the seasonings except for the pepper. Bring to a boil, then reduce the heat and cook it all at a simmer until the potatoes are done.
3. Purée the soup in a blender, then return to the soup pot and add the warmed milk and the white pepper. Heat gently without boiling, and serve. We enjoy this and all creamed soups with dumplings and/or biscuits (see the Tofu Pot Pie recipe, page 99 about making dumplings).

Serves six to eight.

*In this and other cream soups it is important to warm the milk or soymilk before adding it to the soup to prevent it from separating.

Cream of Spinach Soup

Spinach makes a natural cream soup. Take it easy with the white pepper with this one--a little goes a long way.

1 large onion, chopped
2 medium potatoes, peeled and chopped
3 cups water
2 tsp. salt
1 pound spinach, cleaned and stemmed
6 medium cloves garlic, peeled
1 1/2 cups hot milk or soymilk.
A pinch each white pepper and nutmeg

1. Sauté the onion in a bit of water until it is very well cooked.
2. Add the three cups water and the potatoes, bring to a boil, and cook at a simmer until the potatoes are tender.
3. Stir in the spinach, garlic, and salt, and purée everything in a blender.
4. Return the puree to the soup pot, add the hot milk and other seasonings, and heat gently without boiling until serving time.

Serves four to six.

Cream of Tomato

Were you one of those kids who grew up on tomato soup and grilled cheese sandwiches? No soup could ever be as good as your Mom's, we know, but this one may run a close second.

2 onions, chopped
1 large potato, peeled and thinly sliced
1 stalk celery, minced
2 cloves garlic, minced
2 cups water
1 28 oz. can whole tomatoes
1 tsp. brown sugar

1 1/2 tsp. salt
1 tsp. dill
1 tsp. thyme
1/4 cup fresh basil
    (or 2 tsp. dried)

1 cup hot milk or soymilk

1. Cook the tomatoes in their juice for about fifteen minutes, and then purée them in the liquid.
2. Bring the water, onion, potato, celery and garlic to a boil in a soup pot. Simmer until the potato is tender.
3. Add the tomatoes and seasonings and simmer for a few more minutes, then stir in the hot milk and serve.

Serves six.

*You can use fresh tomatoes if you have plenty in your garden. See the How To section for how to peel them.

Corn and Baby Lima Bean Chowder

Based on an old Southern favorite, this soup is hard to beat when made with fresh corn. Try serving it with biscuits and a tofu spread made with fresh basil.

1 1/2 cups dry baby lima beans
1 medium potato, diced
2 onions, chopped
3 cloves garlic, minced
3 stalks celery, minced
1 tsp. basil
1/2 tsp. thyme
3 cups corn
4 cups hot milk or soymilk
1/4 tsp. black pepper.
1-2 tsp. salt

1. Soak the beans overnight. When you are ready to make the soup, cook them very gently in fresh water until they are just tender.
2. Cook the potato in boiling water until just tender. Drain well, and set aside.
3. Meanwhile, sauté the onion, garlic, celery, salt, and herbs in a bit of water until the onion is very tender.
4. Add the corn and cook about ten minutes more.
5. Add the cooked beans, potatoes, milk, salt and pepper. Heat gently without boiling, and serve.

Serves six.

Winter Squash Soup

If you tell yourself that you don't like winter squashes, don't believe it. There is a conspiracy against this yummiest of all vegetables. Try this, or one of the other squash soups in this book, and it'll make a monk out of you.

1 onion, chopped
4 cloves garlic, minced
6 cups baked and puréed winter squash (butternut, acorn, etc.)*
2 cups (or more) water
2 tsp. dried basil
2 tsp. salt
3 cups hot soymilk (unsweetened preferably)

1. Sauté the onion and garlic in a little water until soft.
2. Add remaining ingredients and heat thoroughly.

Serves eight.

*See the How To section for how to cook winter squashes.

Yellow Split Pea-Squash Soup

2 cups yellow split peas

8 cups water

1 cup sliced celery

1 cup sliced carrot

3 cloves garlic, minced

1 onion, chopped

2 bay leaves

1 tsp. basil

1/4 tsp. pepper

1/2 tsp. marjoram

1/4 tsp. cumin

1 15 oz. can whole
   or diced tomatoes

2 tsp. salt

4 cups cooked, puréed
   winter squash (acorn,
   butternut, etc.)*

1. Place all the ingredients except the tomatoes, salt, and squash in a soup pot and bring to a boil. Lower heat and simmer until the peas are very tender (an hour or more).

2. Add the tomatoes and salt and cook for ten more minutes. Stir in the squash and add water if necessary. Serve hot.

Serves eight to ten.

*See the "How To" section for how to cook winter squashes.

Yellow Split Pea-Vegetable Soup

Yellow split peas make a wonderful soup base. If you cook them long enough (over an hour), they disintegrate into a yellow broth that takes to just about any vegetable and seasonings. This is just one of the pea soups that we eat regularly--try the others in this book, as well, for a different flavor.

3 cups yellow split peas

10 cups water

2 onions, chopped

8 cloves garlic, minced

1/2 head cauliflower, in one-inch pieces

1 pound broccoli, in one-inch flowerettes

2 leeks

1 28 oz. can diced tomatoes

1 1/2 tsp. paprika

3 to 4 tsp. salt

1 tsp. pepper

3 bay leaves

1 1/2 tsp. thyme

1/2 pound frozen peas

1. Place the split peas and water in a pot and bring to a boil. Reduce heat and simmer until the peas are very tender, an hour or more.
2. Sauté the onions and garlic in water until the onions are translucent, about five minutes.
3. Add the cauliflower and broccoli, leeks, tomatoes, and seasonings; cover, and cook over low heat until all the vegetables are tender (ten minutes or so).
4. Add the cooked split peas and the green peas, bring to a simmer, and serve.

Serves eight to ten.

Split Pea Soup
(adapted from The Peaceful Palate)

We have a tradition of serving this soup on the first evening of big retreats as a way to welcome our guests after their often long journeys to the Monastery. It's a natural with cornbread and Tomato and Avocado Salad.

2 cups split peas, rinsed
6 cups hot water
1 cup carrots, diced or sliced
1 cup celery, sliced
1 medium to large onion, chopped
2 garlic cloves, minced or pressed
1/2 tsp. marjoram
1/2 tsp. basil
1/4 tsp. cumin
1/4 tsp. coarsely ground pepper
pinch cayenne pepper
1 tsp. salt

1. Sort and rinse the split peas and place them in a large kettle with all the other ingredients except the salt.
2. Bring to a simmer, then cover loosely and cook until the peas are tender, about one hour. When the peas are cooked, add the salt.

Serves six.

Red Lentil and Squash Soup

If you have never cooked with red lentils, don't wait any longer. This bright orange legume is popular in the Middle and Far East, and with good reason. The recipe that follows is an adaptation of a traditional Masoor Dal recipe (a "dal" is an Indian "bean dish"). We had a hunch that red lentils and squash would be a magical marriage, and sure enough. You can find red lentils at most natural food stores.

3 cups (or more) cooked and puréed butternut or other winter squash
1 cup red lentils
6 cups water
1 quarter-sized slice fresh ginger
1 tsp. turmeric
1/2 tsp. whole cumin seed, toasted in a dry pan
1 tsp. salt

1. Bake the squash,* scoop the meat out of the shell, and purée.
2. While the squash is baking, wash the lentils and put them in a big pot with the water. Bring to a boil and skim off the foam
3. Add the ginger, turmeric, and cumin seed. Cook until the lentils are tender (45 minutes or so).
4. Add the salt and the puréed squash and more water if needed.
5. Heat thoroughly and serve.

Serves six to eight.

*see the How To section for cooking winter squash.

Black Bean Soup

2 cups dry black beans

2 onions, chopped

8 cloves garlic, minced

2 carrots, diced

1-2 green or red bell peppers, diced

1 28-ounce can diced tomatoes and juice

1/4 tsp. black pepper

2 tsp. cumin

2 tsp. salt

1 1/2 cups orange juice

1. Sort the beans and soak them overnight. When it is time to make the soup, drain the beans, put them in a pot and add enough fresh water to cover by at least two inches, and cook them until they are tender but are still able to hold their shape. Drain the beans, saving the cooking liquid.

2. Sauté the onion, garlic, and carrot in a bit of water until everything is almost tender. Add the bell pepper and tomatoes and seasonings and cook for another five minutes.

3. Add the vegetables to the bean pot along with the orange juice and enough of the cooking liquid to make it a soup. Simmer for another minute, and serve. We like to put out sour cream and salsa as garnishes with this soup.

Serves six to eight.

Minestrone

This is a good way to use up leftover odds and ends.

3 cups onions, chopped
3 cloves garlic, minced
2 stalks celery, sliced
2 carrots, sliced
2 tsp. basil
1 tsp. oregano
1 bay leaf
1 tsp. salt
1/4 tsp. pepper
1 28 oz. can of tomatoes, chopped
4 cups vegetarian broth (made with bouillon)
3 to 4 cups of greens, potatoes, beans, pasta, or any combination of leftovers
Parmesan cheese (optional)

1. Steam (or sauté in small amount of water) onions, garlic, celery, and carrots until onions are soft.
2. Add basil, oregano, bay leaf, salt, and pepper and sauté for another one to two minutes.
3. Add canned tomatoes, broth, and greens, potatoes, etc. Three cups will make a thinner soup; four cups will make a soup with more of a stew-like consistency. Serve with Parmesan cheese (optional).

Serves eight.

Miso-Onion Soup

You've got to really appreciate that most humble of all vegetables, the onion, to enjoy this soup, but if you do, you'll love it. Some people like a very strong miso flavor and others don't, so you can add or subtract to suit your tastebuds.

4 onions, sliced
4 cloves garlic, sliced
1/4 cup peeled and sliced ginger
8 cups water (or more)
10 Tbs. miso
1 pound tofu, in half inch cubes

1. Sauté the onions, garlic, and ginger in a tiny bit of canola oil until very soft. This will take about ten minutes (it may be necessary to add a little water to keep them from sticking).
2. Add the water and tofu, simmer for five minutes, then turn off the heat.
3. Place the miso in a separate bowl, spoon some of the hot soup broth over it, and whisk until the miso is dissolved. Pour this mixture back into the soup bowl, stir thoroughly, and serve. If the soup needs to be reheated, do not allow it to come to a boil.

Serves eight to ten.

Summer Fruit Soup

Very popular in July and August. The summers here can be a bit warm, to put it mildly, and a gang of sweaty monks can put this cool, colorful soup away by the gallon.

3 cups orange juice
3 cups fat-free yogurt
1 Tbs. fresh lemon juice
1 Tbs. honey
4 cups berries or summer fruit, any type (blueberries, blackberries, strawberries, peaches, nectarines, cantaloupe, cherries), or a mixture
a pinch each of cinnamon and nutmeg

1. Whisk together orange juice and yogurt.
2. Add remaining ingredients and chill until served.

Serves four to six.

Vichyssoise

Any decent French chef would be horrified by this low-fat adaptation of the classic soup, and even more so by the substitution of soymilk for cow's milk, but the result is actually very satisfying. More or less zucchini could be used than the recipe calls for, and chopped fresh spinach could be added either with the zucchini--in which case it would be puréed and turn the soup green--or after the soup has chilled, giving it some added color and texture.

2 onions, chopped
1 pound red or white potatoes, peeled and cut into chunks
1 pound zucchini, diced
a large handful of fresh spinach, washed, stemmed, and chopped (optional)
4 cups water
1 1/2 tsp. salt
1/4 cup chopped fresh basil (or 1/2 tsp. dried)
1/8 tsp. white pepper
2 cups milk or soymilk
Optional: fresh basil, dill, parsley

1. Sauté the onions with the salt in a little water until very soft, about ten minutes.
2. Add the water and potatoes and bring to a boil. Reduce heat, cover, and simmer for five minutes.
3. Add the zucchini, optional spinach, and basil. Return to a simmer and cook until everything is tender.

4. Purée everything in a blender until it's all very smooth. Stir in the milk or soymilk and white pepper and chill until very cold (three or four hours) before serving.

Serves six.

A Once in a Lifetime Experience

There is no denying it, we eat well at the Monastery. If breakfast cannot get you disidentified from a suffering place, it may be a long day ahead. Cereals, homemade soymilk, granola, hot oatmeal, a variety of breads and jams, yogurts and cottage cheese, dried fruit, and when it's just the monks--the toaster! It's the best to work in a kitchen that is stocked with all kinds of great foods. There are tubs of organic flours and cereals, jars and jars of beans and grains, not to mention the garden outside the back door, overflowing most of the year with beautiful organic produce of all kinds. Whenever I work in the kitchen, I feel surrounded by abundance.

My stint as the Monastery cook was a relatively short one, but nonetheless lively and colorful. Ask anyone who's been the cook and they will know what I mean. Whenever the cook brings up his or her struggles in a group discussion, all of the former cooks look sideways, their heads nod, a groan or two can be heard. There is an unacknowledged secret society that former cooks all belong to--they have gone through the initiation rites: cooking at Carmel, fine-tuning the art of leftovers, getting nine or more shopping carts through the check out line and loaded in a vehicle, delegating oven space for tonight's cornbread and tomorrow's muffins, packing leftovers in the refrigerators, dealing with ants, and perhaps the biggest of them all--the tomato harvest. It can get kinda nutty in the kitchen, but being the cook is a once in a lifetime experience.

Ultimately, though, the kitchen and all it entails so wonderfully reflects Life. We plan a meal, we buy the food--all with donated money--we prepare it lovingly, we eat, we clean up, we put everything away. When I'm cooking the meals, especially on a retreat, I think of the Tibetan sand mandalas. Here I am creating a mandala with this meal. It reflects all the interconnectedness of life: the farmers who grew the food, the transportation, the donated money, the preparation, all those that made the kitchen equipment, the people who will partake in the eating-- members of Sangha who have come together to practice letting go of suffering, and on and on and on.. The mandala is created with the meal preparation, and with the ringing of the meal bell, like the sand mandala, it falls apart. Letting it go, as the food transforms into nourishment and sustenance, just the next phase in the process of life. And soon we will be scrubbing dishes and packing up the leftovers, putting away food processors and knives, shelving jars of this and that. And as the last monk heads out of the kitchen, the cook can be seen huddled over menus, the catalyst in the mandala coming back together again. May all beings have full bellies and never hunger. May all beings be nourished and live in the full abundance the Earth has to offer.

--from a monk

It's How, Not What

Before I began cooking for Monastery retreats, I cooked at Kripalu Center (a large yoga center in Massachusetts) for 300 to 700 people per meal. We had a team that cooked, a team that prepped veggies, and a team that washed dishes. Even with all these people focused on the same goal--providing good food lovingly prepared in a generous atmosphere--things could still get very intense at times.

In that environment we were often reminded, "It's not about the food." At 11:15, when lunch began at 11:30, it seemed like it was about the food and about getting lunch out on time. But sometimes, even under that kind of pressure, I could see, "It's not about the food, it's about being present to myself and what's going on around me," and the food would get done and out on time.

At the Monastery we practice and cook with the teaching, "It's not what, it's how." If I get caught up in one little thing (obsessing really) about the salad dressing or the dessert, I can lose sight of the whole meal, and then end up behind and late and stressed. The whole work period becomes about me and how things are not going well, instead of about being present to all that goes on within me around preparing a meal, and feeling the energy of life move through me.

I have discovered that getting caught up in something small, or being overly concerned about the end result, leads to the same places: not getting a satisfactory outcome, and not enjoying the process.

These days I teach movement (yoga, pilates, somatics) instead of cooking for retreats. In movement, as in cooking, "how, not what" is important to remember because we tend to get caught up in trying to do a movement and trying to do it right. This is the *what*. The secret to being able to "do it right" lies in forgetting about the finished look of the movement and focusing on the sensation of the muscles being used, the quality of the experience we are having, and whatever else is there in the moment. That is, focusing on the *how*. The interesting thing is that if we stop trying for a particular outcome, we end up with a much better result than if we focus on doing the movement right.

So the movement might look right, and the food might be delicious, ample, and done on time. But if not, we'll have learned so much, and been so present with ourselves, that we'll feel good and alive. And that's all cooking and movement and practicing is about, feeling alive and present. And how, not what, gets me that.

--from a retreatant

The Pupil and the Black Pot

It is the biggest pot I have ever seen.
It is the heaviest pot I have ever lifted.
It can feed a biblical number of people.
It can empty in an awesomely short amount of time.
It can glisten incredibly tempting.
It's one of the kitchen cornerstones.
It's one of the mute role models of monastic life,
never complaining, always ready to serve, a forever
forgiving teacher.

It has seen a lot.
It has helped countless pupils cook their Karma and watch it slowly evaporate, drop by drop.
It has also seen me when I first came to the Monastery kitchen.

I struggled with every single task, afraid that I would ruin whatever I was assigned to do, should it be as simple as prepping lettuce. I prepped lettuce for about a month before I was shifted to prepping veggies. It took about two months for me to find a rhythm of chopping onions--onions that always disappeared into the Black Pot and ended up in a miraculous meal. Then I was assigned to prepare my first dessert.

It was a disaster. A complete disaster. A silent internal chaotic turmoil disaster, stirring up thoughts I had no idea even existed, the kind of disastrous disaster that can only be experienced in this Monastery kitchen.

The only one I dared confess to was the Black Pot. It learned that I had mistaken baking powder for baking soda, not sifted the white flour because I had been too proud to inquire about the meaning of "sift" (English is not my native language), and above all had taken the wrong amount of water for the egg replacer liquid because I got confused about the sum of "one-eighth of a teaspoon times 3.5." But the Black Pot remained silent and seemed fairly unimpressed at all the mess I had created, unlike the raging voices inside my head. Actually, neither the Pot nor anyone else said anything at all. Nothing happened except for the outrageous thought (that seemed like a huge risk to believe), "I might live through this and I might not be alone in it."

Many lettuce leaves later, on a sunny September morning of retreat preparation, the Cook was needed at the other end of the property and asked me to finish Sunday lunch.

Before I knew it, I was alone with Chunky Tomato Sauce and Meatball instructions. Time was tight. I neither knew where to find all of the ingredients nor did I understand every single word in the recipe, but, opposite to countless previous attempts, I just kept going, trusting it would work out somehow. And it did. Independent from the fairly acceptable result, it worked because I did not make succeeding or failing mean anything. For the first time, it was just chopping and cooking and dishes. What a relief.

While I was stirring the sauce one last time, looking at the vivid color inhabiting the Black Pot, simmering on this huge Monastery kitchen stove, where so many had stood before me, in this very kitchen and in many Monastery kitchens before my time, I was proud as never before in my adult life.

Finally, I had become a pupil.

--from a former monk

Salads

Anybody can make a salad. Anybody can make a really good salad, for that matter, but it takes a certain amount of sensitivity. You can tell the skill of a cook by the salad he or she makes. If you are served a delicately made salad at the beginning of a meal, you can be sure that whatever follows will be excellent as well. We eat salad by the truck-load here. Last spring, the gardener (who was new to the job and a bit over-enthusiastic) set out four hundred lettuce plants in March. Just about anywhere else, most of them would have bolted and gone to waste before they could be consumed, but the monks rose to the occasion, and we ate every one. For many of us here it's not possible to have too much.

Salad making is a creative endeavor. The best salads come from the heart or the gut and not from the head, and for this reason we have avoided including many green salad recipes. You can't really tell somebody how to make a great salad--they have to find out for themselves. This section contains recipes that mostly involve particular types of salads (cabbage salads, Waldorf salads, cucumber salads, etc.), leaving you all by your lonesome when it comes to what most people think of when they hear the word "salad." Here are a few suggestions, however, to get you started.

As always, use only the best vegetables and salad greens you can find. Many types of lettuces exist other than the two or three commonly found in supermarkets. If you are lucky enough to have a source for them, it's lovely to buy several types at once and mix them together in the bowl. All the different colors and flavors are very appealing that way. We like to mix a bunch of types of seeds together when we sow them in our garden so we can harvest them as a mixture right there. Some people like to mix bitter greens, such as arugula, with the lettuce in their salads, and others most definitely don't, so you'll have to try and see what you fancy. Fresh spinach makes a wonderful salad, either alone or mixed with lettuce. Baby chard works well also, although a salad made only with chard may present a challenge to somebody who is used to iceberg lettuce.

Just about any vegetable that can be eaten raw will be good in a salad. We prefer to lightly steam broccoli and cauliflower for salads. It's fine to use it raw, but it's a good idea to cut it into very small pieces if you do. Some cooked

Vegetables will do fine as well. Thinly sliced cooked beets, for example, are a wonderful addition to a salad (careful, though, they will turn your salad an unpleasant pink color if they are tossed too much with the lettuce).

Here are some things that we enjoy in salads: toasted sunflower or sesame seeds, toasted nuts, croutons, raisins or other dried fruit, thinly sliced red onion, artichoke hearts (packed in water, not oil), cooked kidney beans and chickpeas. Tofu is also good in salads, especially if it has been marinated first in some sort of flavorful dressing. A nice thing to do with leftover steamed vegetables is to marinate them in your favorite dressing and then toss them in with the salad at the last minute, dressing and all.

The two things to consider when planning a salad are its appeal to the eye and the textures it will have when it is being eaten. Cut up your vegetables carefully and artfully. Big chunks of raw carrot or summer squash, for example, will make a salad uncomfortable to eat, but grated carrot or paper-thin slices of squash will be lovely. In general, the more difficult a vegetable is to chew, the smaller the pieces should be. Grate red cabbage, but leave fresh tomatoes in gigantic wedges when you are lucky enough to have them. Tear the lettuce into pieces that are small enough to go easily into your mouth. A good rule of thumb when it comes to vegetables in salads is: too little rather than too much. A thin slice of red pepper here, a kidney bean there, with perhaps a few sunflower seeds and carrot shavings around

are often all that you need. Do something different every time; surprise yourself with the possibilities that are available. Keep in mind the colors of the vegetables that you choose as well and your salads will be very beautiful.

A word about salad dressings:

Most of the dressings you will find in traditional cookbooks will be very high in fat. This is a difficult area in low-fat cooking, but with a little persistence and a few tricks, you can make very good salad dressings with only a fraction of the ordinary fat. The easiest thing to do is merely to substitute water for the oil in the recipe you are experimenting with. The result will possibly not be what you are used to, but you may like it anyway. Dressings made this way will be very thin. To compensate for this, try this trick: Stir a teaspoon of cornstarch into a cup of water, bring it to a boil on the stove, simmer for one minute, and then allow it to cool. The resulting liquid will resemble oil in consistency and can be used rather than water as a substitution in recipes (many commercial fat-free dressings are made this way). Low-fat or fat-free dairy products can be used to make salad dressings as well, especially buttermilk. Even if a recipe does not call for dairy, you can try substituting milk, buttermilk, or soymilk for the oil to make a creamy version, particularly if it involves things like tomato paste or avocados. There are some fat-fee and low-fat types of mayonnaise on the market that are not bad at all, although they tend to contain a lot of sugars. Seasoned rice vinegar can also be used as a substitute for oil (or all by itself--it's very mild and tasty). A very interesting way to make dressings is to put a little tofu in a blender and drizzle in soymilk until the consistency resembles mayonnaise, add a bit of salt and lemon juice and some seasonings, and there you are. And there are, of course, any number of commercial low-fat dressings available; they range from pretty good to pretty bad, with most of them falling on the pretty good side.

You will hear people say that making a fresh salad is just too much trouble, but what this says to us is that they consider themselves to be too much trouble. Treat yourself to a great big salad whenever you can, whether you think you deserve it or not. It's one of the best ways you can take care of yourself.

Super Salad with Broccoli, Walnuts, & Feta Cheese

A lot of people would call this a Greek Salad. We have a tradition that goes beyond anyone's memory of serving this salad with baked potatoes and fixings for our evening meal. It's like cereal and milk-- that's just what you do.

1 head leaf lettuce
1/2 cup red onion, thinly sliced
1 small (or 1/2 large) red bell pepper, halved and sliced
1/4 pound broccoli flowerettes
2 oz. feta cheese, crumbled
1/2 cup walnuts, toasted and chopped

1. Steam the broccoli for one minute. Let cool and toss with the rest of the ingredients.

Serves five or six.

Raw Carrot Beet Salad

Our yoga teacher shared this recipe with us. The last instruction was, "Taste and go to heaven." In our experience, this automatically happens. Such a yummy salad, it often doubles as a dessert.

To soak:
1/2 cup dates
1/2 cup raisins
3/4 cup almonds

To combine:
3 cups grated carrots
1 1/2 cups grated beets
1 1/2 cups grated apples
1/2 cup grated sweet potatoes
1/4 cup fresh lemon juice
salt to taste

1. Soak the dates, raisins, and almonds in a container with twice as much water. Refrigerate for 24 hours.
2. After they are finished soaking, drain the fruit and nuts, then purée them in a blender or food processor.
3. Combine the vegetables, apples, lemon juice, and salt in a large bowl. It's good to toss the sweet potatoes and apples with the lemon juice right away after they are grated to prevent browning.
4. Mix everything together and serve.

Serves 6-8.

Curried Spinach Salad

(adapted from <u>The Peaceful Palate</u>)

Fresh spinach greens make a wonderful salad. The combination of the sweet fruit with the sour fat-free dressing makes this one especially good.

1 bunch fresh spinach (about 1 pound)
1 tart green apple, diced
2 green onions, including green tops, finely sliced
1/4 cup golden raisins or dried apricots, coarsely chopped
1/3 cup almonds, toasted and chopped
1 Tbs. sesame seeds, toasted

3 Tbs. seasoned rice vinegar
3 Tbs. water
2 tsp. stone ground or Dijon style mustard
1 tsp. soy sauce
1 tsp. honey or sugar
1/2 tsp. curry powder
1/4 tsp. black pepper

1. Wash spinach thoroughly, making sure to remove all the sand and grit. The easiest way to do this is to submerge it in a basin of cold water and swish it around. Remove the spinach and replace the water. Repeat until no grit shows up at the bottom of the bowl. Pat spinach dry and tear leaves into bite-sized pieces. Add apple, onion, and raisins or apricots.

2. Toast the almonds and sesame seeds in a dry skillet over medium heat until lightly browned, approximately 5 minutes. Cool and add to the salad.

3. Combine the vinegar, water, mustard, soy sauce, sugar, curry powder, and black pepper. Whisk together. Pour over salad and toss to mix just before serving.

Serves six to eight.

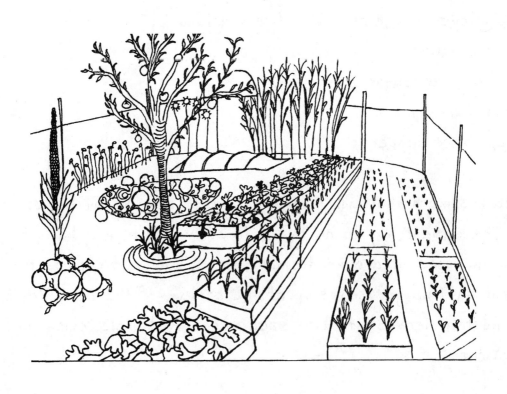

Tomato and Avocado Salad

A very yummy, very popular salad. I think I can speak for everyone here when I say that we just adore avocados, and, if we were rich, we would eat them by the trainload, I'm sure. As it is, they are a treasured commodity, and this is one of our favorite ways to treat ourselves. Please do not do this wonderful fruit the disservice of mixing it with a mealy winter tomato; only straight off the vine organic tomatoes will do.

4 avocados, cut in 1/2 inch cubes
4 medium tomatoes, cut in 1/2 inch pieces
1/2 cup sliced green onion
1/4 cup orange juice
3 tsp. red wine vinegar
1 medium clove garlic, crushed
1/2 tsp. salt
1/4 tsp. black pepper
lettuce

1. Combine avocado, tomato, and green onion slices. Toss gently.
2. In a small bowl, whisk together the remaining ingredients. Mix this dressing gently with the avocado and tomatoes. Chill until serving time.
3. To serve, prepare a bed of lettuce on a platter and mound the avocado-tomato mixture on top.

Serves four.

Waldorf Salads

A "Waldorf" salad is made from a mixture of fruits and vegetables, often with a dairy-based dressing. As with other types of salads in this section, this one lends itself to almost endless variation. So as to avoid robbing you of the pleasure and fun of discovering for yourself all the possibilities that can come together in a Waldorf salad, we thought we would offer you some general guidelines to get you started, but not anything more particular than that. Why not dive right in if you're willing, and just see what happens? It's good practice.

1. Usually the first thing we do when we make a Waldorf salad is to squeeze the juice from a lemon and pour it into the bottom of a large bowl.

2. Next, we might core one or two tart green apples (Granny Smith, for example), cut them into dice-sized cubes, and toss them with the lemon juice to prevent them from browning. This will serve as the base of the salad, you might say. If you use oranges or grapefruits in your salad, you may omit the lemon juice and toss the apples with the citrus instead, as this will have the same effect. Sweet apples could be used instead of tart ones, but their color and texture do not tend to hold up as well.

3. Now comes the fun part: you get to decide from amongst all of the wonderful possibilities what ingredients you will use to create your salad. Here are a few suggestions:

Fruit: Mostly, we prefer to use autumn and winter fruits in our Waldorf salads--oranges, grapefruits, red or green grapes, pears, and pineapple, for example--or, if we're feeling gutsy, papaya or mango. If summertime fruit is available (peaches, nectarines, melons) we will tend to make a fruit salad instead (see the following recipe). Figure on one to two large pieces of fruit per person. The fruit will need to be cut into pieces for the salad, and you will want to do this carefully, carving out any bruised spots, removing all the seeds, and so on. The salad will be more beautiful and pleasant to eat if you leave the pieces large. It is a good idea when preparing citrus fruits for a salad to remove all of the white membrane; to do this, peel the orange or grapefruit with a serrated knife, then cut each section away from the central membrane, so that you finish with the membrane all in one piece in your hand, and a pile of handsome orange or red sections on your cutting board.

Vegetables: Many vegetables will not work well in a Waldorf salad. Imagine putting broccoli and pears together in a salad--not most people's idea of a good time. But if you are both the cook and the diner, then that would be completely up to you. Crunchy things are what will be called for, generally, such as celery, carrots, peppers, or red onion. You will want to be very subtle with your vegetables--slice things thin so they will be easy to chew, and lean towards the side of having too little rather that too much. A sliver of red pepper here, a hint of red onion there, the crunch of minced celery in between, if not overdone, will add wonderfully to the beauty and texture of your salad.

Other things: Most dried fruits will be lovely in your salad--raisins, dates, chopped apricots, cranberries--whatever you like. Just about any nut or seed will improve a Waldorf salad as well, especially if they are toasted first. You might also add chunks of cheese, or, in a spunky moment, slices of avocado. Start small, we recommend, and allow the salad to create itself.

4. As the ingredients of your salad are prepared, toss them in the bowl with the apples. As you go along,, if you attend to the colors and shapes that are being combined this will assist you in the further choices that you make.

5. When you are satisfied that your salad is complete, it is time for the dressing. The easiest way to handle this is to simply toss everything with a spoonful of yogurt or a mixture of yogurt and mayonnaise. If you don't mind a little more of a challenge, however, you might whisk together something slightly more complex, like so:

1 cup yogurt
1/4 cup mayonnaise
1/2 cup orange juice
2 Tbs. honey
a pinch of cinnamon and/or cardamom
a very tiny pinch each of salt and pepper

Toss the dressing with the fruits and vegetables, and serve it on a bed of lettuce.

Here are a couple more ideas to play with:
  --You could grate 5 or 6 carrots and add them to the apples and whatever else you wanted for a carrot salad.
  --You might grate half a head of cabbage and two carrots, and add this to the apples, etc., for a fruity coleslaw (red grapes go especially well with this).

Fruit Salads

One of our favorite summertime evening meals is a big fruit salad, home made yeasted bread, and a spread of some sort. A fruit salad is one of the easiest and most satisfying things you can make-- it is almost guaranteed to be good, no matter what you do. At its simplest, a fruit salad is merely a bowl of cut-up fruit, and even at its most complex, it is not much more than that. Here are a few suggestions to get you started.

Making a fruit salad is much the same as making a Waldorf salad (see the preceding recipe), only it's even easier. When we wish to make a fruit salad here, we most often start in the same way, with the juice of a lemon and a tart apple or two. Toss the apple with the juice in a large bowl to keep it from browning, and toss in the carefully cut fruit as you go. Pretty much any fruit will be wonderful in a fruit salad, as far as we can tell. Our favorites to choose from are oranges and grapefruits, peaches and nectarines, cantaloupe, honeydew, and other melons; watermelon, grapes, pears (as long as they are not over-ripe), and kiwi. We also love berries in our fruit salads, especially strawberries and blueberries. Be sure to cut away any bruised places on your fruit before adding it to the salad and to pick out all the seeds. It's good to keep the apple pieces small (about the size of a dice) because they are more difficult to chew than most other things, but otherwise it is good to keep the slices or chunks of fruit fairly large so that they will retain their distinctiveness in the salad, and so the colors and textures of each will contrast. Apples and pears do not need to be peeled; oranges and grapefruits will be enjoyed the most if the membranes have been cut away from the fruit itself--see the Waldorf salad pages above for a description of how to do this. We recommend that you do not include everything you like in every salad, otherwise they will all be the same. Instead, experiment with different combinations of just a few that you enjoy. A mixture of colors will add to the salad's beauty. Imagine a fruit salad made with apples, peaches, and blueberries; or grapefruit, oranges, red grapes, and perfectly ripe pears.

Dried fruits are very good in fruit salads as well, and so are toasted nuts and seeds. Just about any type of either will do (try poppy seeds, for example). We generally serve our fruit salads without any dressing, but, if you wanted, you could toss yours with a spoonful of yogurt and a little honey. You could turn your fruit salad into hearty a meal with the addition of cottage cheese and perhaps a piece of whole wheat bread on the side.

Cucumber Salad

1/2 red onion very thinly sliced

4 medium cucumbers

1 1/4 cups yogurt

3/4 cup chopped walnuts, lightly toasted

2 small cloves garlic, minced

1 tsp. honey

2 Tbs. freshly minced mint leaves (or 2 tsp. dried)

1/4 cup (packed) finely minced parsley

2 scallions, finely minced

2 Tbs. freshly minced dill (or 2 tsp. dried)

1/4 tsp. black pepper

1 tsp. salt

1. Soak onions in cold water for 30 minutes. Drain and pat dry.
2. Peel and seed cucumbers and cut into thin rounds. Place in a medium-sized bowl.
3. Add remaining ingredients and mix well. Cover and refrigerate until serving time.

Serves six.

Basic Coleslaw

Dill is a natural in slaw, especially if you are lucky enough to have fresh dill in your garden. This recipe is very open-ended; no two slaws need ever look alike, and you can use the suggested variations to discover what you like best. Use both red and green cabbage, if you like. A word of caution, though: Not everything on the list will go well with everything else so, if you're cooking for company, you might want to keep it simple until you're certain what you're doing.

1 head cabbage, shredded and minced
6 carrots, grated
1/2 cup mayonnaise

1/2 cup cider vinegar
1 1/2 tsp. salt
2 Tbs. dill

1. Combine all ingredients and chill.

Vegetable Variations: peppers, corn, green beans, cauliflower, broccoli, celery, and just about anything else; grated, minced, or cut into small chunks.

Fruit Variations: (omit dill) grated apples, pineapple, raisins, dates, dried apricots. Good with cardamom.

Nuts and Seeds Variations: sunflower seeds, poppy seeds, walnuts, or almonds; one-fourth to one-third cup per recipe.

Serves about eight.

Fruity Carrot Salad

In the middle of the summer here, when it just gets too hot for hot soups, we start pulling out recipes like this one for the evening meal. It will make a refreshing light supper when served with fresh bread, a spread, and perhaps some lettuce and tomatoes from the garden.

2 pounds carrots, grated (a food processor works well for this)
5 oz. whole pitted dates, cut into thirds
1 fifteen-ounce can pineapple chunks, drained
3/4 cup raisins
1/2 cup toasted almonds, chopped
pineapple juice plus orange juice to make 1 cup
a pinch of salt
2 Tbs. sugar
1/2 tsp. almond extract

1. Combine the carrots, fruit, and nuts in a bowl.
2. In another bowl, combine remaining ingredients and stir to dissolve the sugar.
3. Stir everything together and chill.

Serves ten.

Black Beans and Corn Salad

This main-dish salad makes a great summertime lunch. It's good with rice or cornbread and tortilla chips, and we like to serve it with lots of fixin's (salsa, grated cheese, sour cream, avocado, chopped green onion, etc.). Be careful not to overcook the beans. The salad will be a lot more appealing if they hold their shape.

2 cups dried black beans
2 cups cooked corn
3 cloves garlic, minced
1/2 red onion, minced
2 large red bell peppers, minced
2 Tbs. olive oil
1/2 cup fresh lime juice (3 to 4 limes)
2 tsp. whole cumin seeds
1/2 cup minced fresh parsley
1 tsp. salt
1/4 tsp. pepper

1. Cook the beans very gently until they are tender but not mushy (see the How To section for details). Drain and rinse in cold water.
2. In a large bowl, combine beans, cooked corn, minced garlic, red onion, bell pepper, salt, olive oil and lime juice.
3. Roast the whole cumin seeds in a dry cast iron skillet over medium heat, stirring constantly, for several minutes, and add them to the salad along with the parsley and black pepper. Mix gently, and serve.

Serves eight to ten.

Nutty Rice Salad

This is another main-dish salad that has been popular for many summers at the Monastery. We like to serve it with oven-roasted beets and green beans or a green salad.

1/2 cup uncooked brown rice

1/4 cup uncooked wild rice

1/2 tsp. salt

1/2 cup almonds, toasted

5 Tbs. currants

1 orange, juiced

1 small diced fennel bulb

1 crisp apple

1. Cook the brown rice and 1/4 teaspoon salt in a cup of water for 45 minutes.
2. Rinse the wild rice. Soak in water for half an hour, then drain. Cook in one cup water with 1/4 teaspoon salt for at least an hour, or until the rice grains are swollen and tender but still chewy. Pour into a colander and drain.
3. Preheat the oven to 350°. While the wild rice is cooking, toast the almonds in the oven for seven to ten minutes, then chop. (If chopped while still warm, they are softer and easier to chop.)
4. Soak the currants in orange juice.
5. Prepare the dressing (see recipe next page).
6. Add the soaked currants and fennel to the warm rice and toss with the dressing.
7. Just before serving, cut the apple into small pieces and add to the rice along with the almonds. Season with salt and pepper if needed.

Serves four to six.

Nutty Rice Salad Dressing

Peel from 1 orange, grated
4 Tbs. fresh orange juice
4 tsp. lemon juice
1 tsp. balsamic vinegar
1/2 tsp. salt
4 scallions, minced
1/4 tsp. fennel seeds, crushed
1 Tbs. chervil or fennel leaves, chopped
1 Tbs. parsley, finely chopped
1/2 tsp. walnut oil

1. Mix all ingredients together and toss with Nutty Rice Salad.

Serves four to six.

Simple Fat-Free Dressing
(adapted from <u>The Peaceful Palate</u>)

You wouldn't think that something so simple could be so good, but it is.
We try to keep a bottleful of this dressing available on the serving
table all the time. Seasoned rice vinegar is available at most
supermarkets, often in the Oriental foods section.

1/2 cup seasoned rice vinegar
1-2 tsp. Dijon mustard
1 clove garlic, pressed

Whisk all ingredients together. This dressing will keep indefinitely in the
refrigerator.

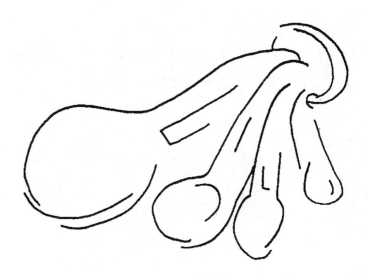

Lemon-Thyme Dressing

This dressing goes extremely well with Mjeddrah (see the Main Dish section).

1 tsp. olive oil
1 1/2 tsp. lemon peel, grated
1/4 cup lemon juice
1 clove garlic, minced
1 1/4 tsp. honey
3/4 tsp. dried thyme leaves
1/2 tsp. salt
dash coarsely ground black pepper
1/4 cup parsley, finely chopped

1. Combine all ingredients except parsley in a blender and blend well. Add parsley just before serving.

Makes half a cup.

The First Thing That Happens

The first thing that happens when you come to the Monastery is that they start making you do stuff. They'll usually take it easy with you in the beginning-- you may find yourself washing windows or sweeping the porches or cleaning the shoe racks or whatever, and you may even have the good fortune of being able to continue in this way for quite some time, but sooner or later it will come to a dismal end: sooner or later they'll ask you to make granola.

"What's so bad about that?" you might say. Well, there's sweeping the porches and then there's making granola. It's not the same thing. I can sweep the porches (especially our porches), and when I'm through, it's impossible to tell if I've done a bad job or a good job. You can always say (or you could if we were allowed to say anything) that that clod of dirt was tracked onto the porch <u>after</u> you had finished--"It isn't <u>my</u> responsibility." Not so with the granola--there's just so much that could go wrong. You could forget about it and it could burn, you could stir it at the wrong time and it could burn, you could fail to stir it properly and it could burn--any way you look it, it could burn. And if it burns, everyone will know you are a BAD PERSON.

The first time, I nearly refused. "How can they ask me to do this?" I asked myself. "This is totally unreasonable." It started looking like my days at the Monastery were over, but then I remembered that I had nowhere else to go (a tremendous advantage in spiritual practice), and so I gave it a try. And I didn't burn it, by a miracle. I crawled quickly back into my hole, but it didn't last long, because the next thing I knew they asked me to bake a cake. I went to my hermitage in a state, and I packed my bags in the night, but I had to unpack them when I remembered I didn't have any money for a plane ticket (another tremendous advantage in spiritual practice). The cake, by a miracle, did not fall or burn or slide onto the floor when I took it out, and was even not too bad to eat. "Okay," I thought, "I've done a cake. No more cakes." But then they asked me-- you're not going to believe this--to prepare a whole lunch. I was down in the parking lot before I realized that I did not have a car to drive away in (yet another tremendous advantage in spiritual practice), and so I stayed and tried it, and, by a miracle, I did it and nothing burned and it was done in time and tasted pretty good, I thought.

Then they made me the Cook, of all things. Friends, I desperately did not want to be the Cook. I would have done anything--anything--so long as it wasn't to be the Cook. I wanted to sweep the porches (especially those porches) for the rest of my days. But then I was on to their little game by this point: they wanted me to prove to myself that I could do it, and that there wasn't any reason for the fear. Well, okay. Worth a try. Looking back I realize that I could have just burned everything and that would have taken care of it, but I didn't think of it, luckily. So I tried, and, by a miracle, I did fine--more than fine, I did well. I figured that must be the end of it, but no. Running out of kitchen challenges, I suppose, they asked me before long to facilitate groups. Next they asked me to travel across the country and cook for away retreats. After that they asked me to facilitate There is Nothing Wrong With You retreats.

Each time I thought to myself, "Well, at least this is it. There isn't anything else they can ask me to do." But there always was something else. I'm certain now that there will always be something else. And every time it turned out okay, by a miracle. After a very long time I got to the place where I could cook for my fellow monks and our visitors without fear, and that's when they gave the job to somebody else and gave me an even worse job. It's been relentless. But what I found out while this went on is that they were right--that I can do it, whatever it is. This is the reason they tortured me so with their little game. I have learned, by a miracle, that there never was any reason to be afraid.

--from a monk

This Will Never Work

The Guide's consistent commitment to the facets of the practice that make it both wholly Zen and wholly unique is one of the things that has always struck me as extraordinary about this practice. I am referring to the concept and structure of the privileged environment; the commitment to offer training to anyone who sincerely wishes to practice; and the unwavering focus on providing nutritious, low-fat, delicious food regardless of where a retreat may be held. This cookbook is the Zen Monastery Cookbook, but it contains recipes used year after year in North Carolina at Nantahala, Penland, and Southern Dharma; at the Kearns Spirituality Center and Franciscan Center in Pittsburgh, Pennsylvania; and at the Sisters of Notre Dame Villa Angelica in Carmel.

Over the years, it has not mattered that circumstances often have been less than ideal for providing meals to twenty or thirty or forty people. Once, we cooked at a retreat center in North Carolina that was still under construction. In the agreement, the owner promised that it would be ready, but, in fact, they had barely begun to build. When we arrived, the "kitchen" had no counters, a single apartment-size stove, a single refrigerator, and virtually no pots and pans. But meals were prepared and served. It seemed as though all the retreatants found the willingness not only to endure surroundings that made wilderness campsites look like luxury accommodations, but also to pitch in and make a successful retreat possible. And the food was great!

Then there was the year when our annual retreat at the beautiful Nantahala Lodge was canceled because the lodge had burned to the ground. However, the next year our generous hosts and devoted Sangha members, Jan and John, arranged to have the retreat by making several condominiums and cottages available. The condos had only apartment-style kitchens, but there were four of them, plus a small kitchen in a cabin the Cook occupied.

Time after time my spiritual practice has been enhanced by the incredible opportunity to be the Cook at retreats like this one. I walk in and my "WRONG" subpersonality (voice in my head) starts in with "This will never work! No way. It can't be done." (This subpersonality lost much of its power the day I walked into a different retreat kitchen with that attitude, and Christa, co-cook and Yoga teacher, said, "Oh, this is great! We can do it." Talk about opposing attitudes! Mine was "WRONG," hers was "GREAT.") Well, there we were with four kitchens in two two-story condos. And I really believed it couldn't be done. But it worked--the retreatants were incredibly helpful, as they always are, and we all got super cardio-vascular workouts running up and down stairs. And, again, the food was great.

We have wonderful recipes to work with and a dedicated group of monks and retreatants who are willing to show up and participate. In the face of all that goodness, it is much easier not to believe my it-won't-work voice.

--from a monk

Because That's What You've Been Practicing

The best part about being the Monastery Cook is that you get to travel to far-off places with Cheri to help out with the away retreats. Everyone should have this experience. The first several times I was asked to do this, it terrified me, but now I find it thrilling. Just imagine: You haven't left the Monastery property for weeks, haven't even seen a dollar bill or somebody wearing a suit, haven't smelled perfume in who knows how long. Suddenly, there you are on a highway with four lanes on each side; in the airport; in the airplane (God save us) being catapulted across the country to foreign lands such as North Carolina; and you are there experiencing the excitement of it all because you are a monk and that's what you've been practicing. You crash (that is, you go to sleep) for a few hours, then you get up, meditate, and you're off on your adventure again.

My favorite part is when I walk into the grocery store I've chosen (in whatever strange town I find myself) and survey the scene, knowing that the people there have no idea who this fanatic is who has dropped in on them out of nowhere and the damage he'll do before he leaves. At first , you may get an odd look or two because of the beads we wear, but that's it. It doesn't take long to start raising eyebrows, though. "Let's see... thirty-seven heads of lettuce--check. Forty pounds of bananas--check. Twenty-five pounds of onions--check." Usually, people think I work for the store, and they start asking me where to find things. The funny thing is that I usually know. I like the part, too, where you negotiate with the produce guy for bargains: "You'll give me ten percent off if I buy a case of tofu? What if I buy ten cases?" The last time, in Asheville, the produce manager had dreadlocks and a big rasta hat (this was a very hip supermarket), and he never blinked an eye--it was amazing. By the time I'm through (three hours later), I've got heaping shopping carts all over the store, and the other shoppers are carefully staying out of my way. I usually play the sedate monk and give obscure answers to people's inquiries. It adds to the effect.

Then you get serious and haul off all that food, get it organized, and start cooking like crazy. Time is usually very tight. The confidence it takes to pull it off (for me) is incredibly intoxicating. Then people you love start arriving and help out. Then more people you love arrive and help out too, and you begin having a wonderful time. Then the teacher you love arrives, and she is very excited about everything and is cracking jokes, and it's just the best. So you cook like crazy for days, and you practice being in the moment with all these lovely people, and when it's all over and everything is cleaned up and everybody is gone, you go for a long, quiet walk by yourself. And while you're walking, you are full of appreciation for yourself for all that you did. You are full of love and gratitude for you and for your life because that is what you've been practicing. And you go home very happy to be a monk. That's really the best part, I guess.

--from a monk

Breads

If you're looking for something to help people feel welcome, it's hard to beat fresh, homemade bread. For many, it's the most basic comfort food. We've noticed that you've got to be very determined if you want to maintain a feeling of unhappiness or dissatisfaction with life when you've got a hot muffin in your hands, or if you're about to dive into a stack of blueberry pancakes, so there is a lot of incentive to keep our serving tables loaded with baked treats. This and the next section contain some of our favorites.

There are two basic types of breads: those made with yeast, and those made with baking powder and/or baking soda, often called "quick breads" or "soda breads." The process of making yeasted breads is somewhat involved and is described in detail in the next section. Soda breads are easier and quicker to make, and the following recipes are mostly self-explanatory, but we thought we might include a few pointers here for those new to baking, in case they are helpful.

Measuring Ingredients

Whether you are making a quick bread, cookies, or a cake, it is important to measure the ingredients very carefully. To this end, it is helpful to choose the measuring cup or spoon that will give you the most accurate measurement. Usually this means that you will want the cup or spoon that is closest to the quantity that you would like to measure. For example, you would not use a four-cup measure to measure 1 3/4 cups of flour. This would require you to do a lot of squinting and would only give you an approximation. If, instead, you use a one-cup measure, a half-cup measure, and a quarter-cup measure, you will end up with a very accurate measurement. The same goes for wet ingredients such as milk or applesauce. If you need four cups, use a four-cup measure; if you need three cups, use a one-cup measure three times. A good technique for measuring dry ingredients, like flour, is to dip the measuring cup into the flour and scrape the excess off the top with a knife. It is especially important to measure baking powder and soda carefully. A little too much or a little too little can make a big difference.

Mixing and Baking

You will notice that the ingredients in the recipes that follow are divided into those that are wet (like milk) and those that are dry (like flour). The basic method is to measure the dry ingredients into one bowl, the wet into another, mix the wet into the dry, pour the batter into the pan, and put it in the oven. The reason it is done this way is that, when baking powder and soda are moistened, the chemical reaction begins to occur that causes the bread to rise. This reaction is fairly short-lived, and you want it to happen in the oven rather than outside it. The process is designed so that you can speedily get the bread batter into the heat once it is mixed. Nothing quite so tests the patience of the cook as when a new monk mixes a batter together, and then leaves to use the facilities or write a note or something before putting the bread in the oven.

Consistency of oven temperature is also important. Give your oven plenty of time to preheat, and open the door as little as possible. It's okay to peek at the bread while it's baking, but make it quick.

Soda bread recipes often tell you to mix the wet and dry ingredients together just until moistened. Too much mixing will produce a tough bread. It's better to have your batter be a little lumpy.

Quick breads generally bake at low temperatures (325°-350°) for a long time, usually fifty minutes to an hour. It is difficult to tell when a loaf is done, but with practice you'll begin to recognize the signs. Most likely it's done if the loaf comes easily out of the pan; if it is brown all over, including the tops and sides; and if it springs back confidently when you poke it on top with your finger. If, in addition to these things, you have measured carefully, have remembered about the oven temperature, and have baked the bread for the required length of time, then you can be sure that it's finished baking. Remove the bread from the oven and allow it to cool on wire racks for ten minutes in the pan, then remove the loaf from the pan to finish cooling.

Biscuits

Making good biscuits is a different thing altogether. The secret is to make them very big and very thick, and to know how much flour to add when you're kneading them to get the right consistency. This is impossible to describe, but when you get it, you'll know it. The other piece is to take them out of the oven at just the right moment, when they are crusty on top but still fluffy in the middle, and to serve them as soon as possible.

Good luck, and enjoy!

BISCUITS (aka: Cat Heads)

Cheri loves her Cat Heads. In some places in the South, a "cat head" is a really, really big biscuit (as big as a cat's head). This recipe will make seven or eight, depending on your cat.

1 1/2 cups unbleached white flour
1/2 cup whole wheat pastry flour
2 tsp. baking powder
1 tsp. salt
1 1/3 Tbs. canola oil
1 cup buttermilk or soymilk

1. Preheat oven to 400°. Sift dry ingredients together.
2. In a separate bowl, combine the oil and buttermilk and mix.
3. Quickly and thoroughly blend the buttermilk mixture with the dry ingredients to form a soft dough. Keep the stirring to a minimum.
4. On a floured board, roll the dough into a 3/4" thick circle and cut into biscuits with a biscuit cutter. Place biscuits on a baking sheet sprayed with nonstick spray.
5. Bake for 15 to 18 minutes, until lightly browned on top.

Makes 7 or 8 biscuits.

*If you don't have a biscuit cutter, don't worry--neither do we. Just take a tin can and cut both the top and the bottom out of it to make your own.

Sweet Potato Biscuits

Two of the best things in the world, sweet potatoes and biscuits, meet in one recipe. This idea came to us from a book with a large section devoted to Caribbean cooking.

1 cup all-purpose flour	3/4 cup mashed cooked sweet potatoes
3/4 cup whole wheat flour	
1 Tbs. baking powder	3/4 cup skim milk (or soymilk)
1/4 tsp. salt	1 1/2 Tbs. vegetable oil

1. Preheat oven to 450°. Spray a baking sheet with nonstick spray.
2. In a large bowl, combine both types of flour, baking powder, and salt. Mix well..
3. In another bowl, combine sweet potatoes, milk and oil, and mix well.
4. Stir the wet ingredients into the dry ingredients. You'll want to keep the stirring to a minimum. It's fine if everything is not completely combined.
5. Place dough on a floured surface and knead a few times until dough holds together in a ball. It's okay to add a little more flour if needed, but keep in mind that the moister the dough, the better the biscuits will be.
6. Roll out dough into a one-inch-thick circle, and cut into biscuits with a biscuit cutter. Arrange the biscuits on the prepared baking sheet.
7. Bake for 12 minutes or so, until bottoms of biscuits are lightly browned.

Makes 14 biscuits.

Corn Bread
(from <u>The Peaceful Palate</u>)

1/2 cup unbleached white flour

1/2 cup whole wheat flour

1 cup cornmeal

2 Tbs. sugar

3/4 tsp. salt

1 tsp. baking powder

1/2 tsp. baking soda

1 1/2 cups buttermilk or soymilk

2 Tbs. canola oil

1. Preheat oven to 425°.
2. In a large bowl, sift dry ingredients and blend well.
3. In another bowl, mix the buttermilk and canola oil.
4. Mix the wet ingredients with the dry ingredients until just blended.
5. Spread the batter evenly in an 8x8" baking dish that has been sprayed with nonstick spray. Bake for 20 to 25 minutes.

Serves 6 to 8.

Basic Muffins

Use this recipe to create your own muffins. Mix and match from the additions suggested below, or try something all your own.

1 cup whole wheat pastry flour

1 cup white flour

3/4 tsp. salt

1/4 cup sugar or other sweetener

2 tsp. baking powder

2 eggs

1/4 cup applesauce

3/4 cup milk or soymilk

Additions:

1/2 cup nuts or seeds

1/2 cup chopped apples, chopped figs, dates, apricots, prunes, or berries

1. Preheat oven to 375°. Sift all the dry ingredients together.
2. Separately, beat the eggs and add applesauce and milk or soymilk.
3. Mix wet and dry ingredients and additions, if any. Stir as little as possible. Spoon into muffin tins that have been sprayed with nonstick spray. Bake for 20 to 25 minutes, or until browned top and bottom.

Makes 12 muffins.

Bran Muffins

1 1/2 cups unbleached flour
1 cup bran
1 Tbs. grated orange peel
1 tsp. baking soda
1/4 tsp. salt
1 cup buttermilk (or soymilk with 1 Tbs. vinegar)
1/4 cup light molasses
1/4 cup applesauce

Options: grated carrot, raisins, chopped prunes, sesame seeds, nuts, or grated apple-- up to a cup of any of these per recipe.

1. Preheat oven to 350°. Combine the dry ingredients.
2. Mix together the wet ingredients.
3. Stir together wet and dry and add one or more of the options if you wish. Spray muffin tin with nonstick spray and spoon in mixture.
4. Bake for 25 minutes. Let muffins cool for five minutes before removing from the pan.

Makes 10 to 12 muffins.

Orange Pecan Muffins

The monks know that whenever we will be having visitors, there will be two things to look forward to: we get to sleep a little later, and we get to have muffins for breakfast. This recipe is one of our favorites.

1/2 cup unbleached white flour
1/2 cup wholewheat pastry flour
1 tsp. baking powder
1/2 tsp. salt
1/4 tsp. baking soda
1/3 cup chopped pecans

2 Tbs. brown sugar or maple syrup
1 egg (or egg replacer)
1 tsp. grated orange peel
1/2 cup orange juice

1. Preheat oven to 375°. Mix wet ingredients together thoroughly.
2. Sift dry ingredients together and stir in chopped pecans.
3. Mix wet ingredients with dry just until evenly moist. Spoon into muffin tins that have been sprayed with nonstick spray.
4. Bake for 25 minutes, or until browned on top and bottom.

Makes 6 large muffins.

Maple Buttermilk Muffins
(adapted from <u>Garden Way Bread Book</u>)

1 cup wholewheat pastry flour
3/4 cup white flour
1 1/2 tsp. baking powder
1 tsp. baking soda
1/2 tsp. salt
1/2 tsp. cinnamon

2 eggs (or replacer)
1/3 cup buttermilk, (or soymilk, plus two teaspoons vinegar)
1/4 cup applesauce
1/2 cup maple syrup
1/2 cup chopped pecans or walnuts

1. Preheat oven to 400°. Sift together dry ingredients.
2. Beat eggs and add remaining wet ingredients. Stir in the nuts.
3. Mix together wet and dry ingredients, stirring just until mixed, and spoon into muffin tins sprayed with nonstick spray.
4. Bake for 20 to 25 minutes.

Makes 12 muffins.

Brown Bread
(adapted from <u>The Peaceful Palate</u>)

2 cups wholewheat flour
1 cup unbleached white flour
2 tsp. baking soda
1/2 tsp. salt
1 1/2 cups buttermilk or soymilk
1/2 cup molasses
1/2 cup raisins (optional)

1. Preheat oven to 350°. Sift dry ingredients into a large mixing bowl and stir or whisk until well combined.
2. Thoroughly mix milk and molasses together.
3. Add raisins and wet ingredients to dry ingredients and stir until well combined.
4. Pour into a loaf pan that has been sprayed with nonstick spray and bake 50 minutes to an hour, or until a toothpick inserted into the center comes out clean.

Serves 6 to 8.

Apricot Bread

(from <u>Garden Way Bread Book</u>)

1 cup dried apricots
boiling water
1 egg
2/3 cup maple syrup
2 Tbs. applesauce
1 cup orange juice
grated peel of one orange
1 tsp. Vanilla
1/2 cup chopped nuts

2 cups unbleached white flour
2 tsp. baking powder
1 tsp. baking soda
1 tsp. salt
1/4 tsp. ginger

1. Preheat oven to 350°. Pour boiling water over the apricots, enough to cover them, and let steep about 10 minutes. Drain and chop the apricots.
2. In a large mixing bowl, beat the egg until light and slightly thick.
3. Add the maple syrup, applesauce, orange juice, orange peel and vanilla. Beat well. Stir in the apricots and nuts.
4. Sift together the flour, baking powder, baking soda, salt, and ginger.
5. Fold the flour mixture into the liquids, stirring just enough to mix thoroughly.
6. Pour into a loaf pan sprayed with nonstick spray and bake about one hour, or until the top is springy to the touch.
7. Cool the loaf in the pan for 10 to 15 minutes before removing it to cool on a rack.

Makes one loaf.

Carrot Bread

(adapted from <u>Garden Way Bread Book</u>)

Very yummy. Like carrot cake, only not so sweet.

2 eggs
1/2 cup maple syrup
1/2 cup applesauce
1 tsp. vanilla

1 1/4 cups grated or
   shredded raw carrot
3/4 cup chopped nuts
1/2 cup gold raisins (optional)

3/4 cup unbleached flour
3/4 cup wholewheat pastry
   flour
1 1/2 tsp. baking powder
1/2 tsp. baking soda

1 tsp. ground cinnamon
1/2 tsp. ground ginger
1/2 tsp. salt

1. Preheat oven to 325°. In a mixing bowl, beat the eggs until they are somewhat thickened.
2. Beat in the maple syrup, then the applesauce and vanilla. Stir in the carrots, nuts and raisins, distributing evenly.
3. Sift together the flour, baking powder, soda, cinnamon, ginger and salt. Add to the liquids and fold until just mixed.
4. Pour the batter into a medium loaf pan that has been sprayed with nonstick cooking spray and bake for 45 to 50 minutes, or until the top feels springy. Let it sit in the pan for about 10 minutes before removing it to cool on a rack.

Makes one medium loaf.

Pancakes

Is there anyone who doesn't like pancakes? When we travel to host retreats in other places, we like to send people off on the final morning with blueberry pancakes, tofu-potato scramble, and smoothies. It's easy to face the big world out there after a meal like that.

1 cup wholewheat or wholewheat pastry flour
1/2 cup white flour
1 tsp. salt
2 Tbs. sugar
2 tsp. baking powder
1 egg
1 to 1 1/4 cups milk or soymilk
Optional: berries (up to 1 1/2 cups per recipe)
            nuts (up to 1/4 cup per recipe)

PANCAKES—
YUM!

1. Sift together dry ingredients.
2. Beat together milk and eggs and stir into dry ingredients.
3. Cook in iron skillet using nonstick spray instead of oil. A medium high flame works best: hot enough to sizzle a drop of water, but not so hot that it smokes. Scoop out about one-third of a cup at a time and pour into the hot pan. Cook until the pancake has browned on the bottom and is bubbling in the middle of the uncooked side. When it has, flip it over and cook that side until it's brown also. Keep the finished cakes warm in the oven on its lowest setting until they are all cooked.

Serves 4 or more (makes about 10 pancakes).

French Toast

This works the very best with homemade yeasted bread. Any type will do. This is one of our favorite Saturday night suppers when it's just us and we don't feel like doing something fancy.

2 eggs
1/2 tsp. salt
2/3 cup milk or soymilk
8 slices bread

1. Heat an iron skillet over a medium flame.
2. Beat the eggs (egg replacer will not work), and then add the salt and milk.
3. Spray skillet with nonstick spray, dip a piece of bread in the egg-milk mixture, and fry it until well browned on the bottom side.
4. Flip it and continue cooking until the other side is brown as well. Keep the toast warm in an oven on low while you cook the other pieces of bread.

Serves 4.

Bread Therapy

Looking back over my tenure as the Monastery Cook, one of the many things that strikes me about that experience is the huge debt of gratitude that I owe to all those big, beautiful balls of bread dough that passed through my hands. I'm betting I baked over five hundred loaves all together, and I swear I still appreciate deeply every one. It is extremely humbling to remember all of the emotion that I poured into those doughs--"Bread therapy" is what I called it. Raw, yeasted bread dough is one of the most wonderful things in the world; for me it was often sympathetic friend, therapist, and compassionate facilitator rolled into one. No, more than that--who else in my life has allowed me to pound them the way I pounded all those mounds of rye and pumpernickel? Who else would so generously have permitted themselves to be beaten, slapped, spanked, thrown against the kitchen counter, and torn into little pieces, just for me? When I recall all the repressed anxiety and frustration that was released into the dough all that time, I am amazed, because it was always met with infinite patience, and never with the least sign of resentment or other complaint. Just like the Monastery, come to think of it.

I have thrown my garbage at the Monastery in ten thousand different ways over the years, and it has never once been suggested to me that this means anything about who I am. I have never been told that I should not feel the way I feel, and it has never been implied that I am bad or unfit or that there was anything wrong with me because of the experience that Life had given me in the moment, and what I had done with that. Now, the Monastery has never yielded, either; but come to think of it, neither has the bread. No matter how much you test it, it is what it is, and I am mirrored in that. Just as in the process of pushing against the structure of the Monastery, as I knead the bread I discover what is me and what is not me: the frustration, the anger, the fear is not me--I am the one, I learn, kneading the bread. I suppose I could go even farther and say that the Monastery is shaped by my struggle in the same way that the dough is--something beautiful is the result either way. You have a steaming brown loaf that fills the whole building with its lovely aroma, or you have a community with arms large enough to contain in compassion all that I and the rest of us might bring to it, and more. The more we ask of it, the more it has to give. The compassion arises where the suffering is; the bread rises and my suffering is healed.

I am no longer one who kneads bread, alas, but the world seems to be full of this same compassion. The Earth teaches me now who I am when I take a shovel to it, and so do the nails as I pound them. But I have a special place in my heart for the bread--it was so soft and gentle with me all that time, and yet so immovable. It was a model of what I might myself become, I suppose.

--from a monk

Bread of Life

My experience with making bread is that it contains all the ingredients for a spiritual practice. First, I start out using all different kinds of ingredients. I never know what the content of the bread is going to be until the process has already started, and I'm told by the Cook what we're putting in it that day. So, I can make no assumptions beforehand. And it takes energy to knead the dough, to get it to the right consistency for baking so that it's firm and moist and the elasticity has been brought out; and that takes time and patience and elbow-work. As I'm kneading I'm counting. In order not to be distracted and to focus on really giving my attention to the bread and the kneading I need to be present. Also, the ability to concentrate while working in a kitchen where people are reaching around you, brushing past you, and doing all kinds of activities, requires presence.

And there is no control. As the bread rises, the timing needs to be worked out so that the bread can be punched down at appropriate intervals. Working that into a schedule of other activities-- working meditation projects, sitting meditation, group discussions--gets interesting. Also, I have no control over the ovens--when they're available, which one to use, and how long baking will take. Since the factors over which I have no control are numerous, there is a need for compassionate acceptance of the various undesirable (not as one would like) conditions under which it has to be made. For example, one of these conditions might be baking it in the oven that bakes the outside very quickly and has a tendency to burn the bread. There's also the need to be creative and inventive in caring for the bread in that situation so that it comes out in the best way it possibly can.

And, of course, there is letting go of results. No matter how well I may have done my part in the bread-making, it may come out tasting delicious, or, as has happened, it may come out not being thoroughly baked in the center and being taken off the serving table, being burned on the bottom, or being too dry and crumbly and ending up as bread pudding because no one wants to eat it. That, too, is a spiritual opportunity to not take things personally. There is bread, and there is the bread of life, compassionate awareness.

--From a monk

Drop Biscuits

My favorite cooking story happened during a silent retreat at Nantahala Village, in North Carolina. It was the first retreat after the beautiful, old lodge burned down, and it was being held in a scattered array of buildings, including four condominiums with kitchens. Those kitchens were the facilities we used to cook for some thirty-five retreatants. Two kitchens were upstairs, two downstairs. They had standard-size electric stoves and refrigerators, so the cooking was a total upstairs/downstairs event, with cook and assistants on the move constantly.

We served biscuits one day, along with some other dishes that required oven use--more ovens than the ones in those four condos. So we commandeered the small oven in the cottage where the Cook was staying, which was about a hundred feet from the condos.

It was countdown time to lunch, and the Cook, challenged by keeping track of the five ovens in use, briefly forgot about the biscuits in the far oven. "OH NO! THE BISCUITS!" she yelled, almost silently, as she remembered them. She ran to the cottage and, just in the nick of time, pulled the biscuits from the oven. Cheri happened to be walking by at that moment, and, seeing her, the Cook dashed out onto the porch, biscuits aloft, and whispered loudly, "They didn't burn!" At which point the biscuits slid off the baking sheet onto the porch.

The Cook did not skip a beat. "The porch is really clean. We'll brush them off and call them 'drop biscuits!'"

And they did.

-- from a monk

Basic Yeast Bread Recipe

For the sponge:

    6 cups warm water

    2 Tbs. yeast

    1/2 cup molasses

    2 cups white flour

    6 cups wholewheat flour

For the dough:

    Add: 2 Tbs. salt

        1/3 cup canola oil

        4-5 cups wholewheat flour

    Makes 4 loaves.

The Procedure

To mix the sponge:

First mix together the water, yeast, and molasses in a large bowl. It's important to be very careful about the temperature of the water. If it is too hot it will kill the yeast; if it is too cold the yeast will be sluggish and the bread will not rise correctly. One way to think of it is "warm, but not hot." Test it with your finger or sprinkle a few drops on your wrist. After the first three ingredients are combined, stir very well with a wooden spoon. As you add the flour, before you stir it in, you will notice lots of little bubbles forming. This is an indication that the yeast is alive and happy and ready to go to work. The consistency should resemble thick pancake batter. Your sponge is now mixed. Put it in a warm place and allow the yeast to work for one hour.

To make the dough:

After the hour is over, you will notice (hopefully) that the sponge has risen in the bowl and has become very light and bubbly. It may have even fallen a little in the middle, which is fine. The first thing to do is add the salt and oil and stir these in (and in the process deflate the sponge). Next begin adding the flour one cup at a time, stirring after each addition, until the dough becomes too stiff to stir with a spoon. (This will take around 3 cups of flour.)

Now it's time to knead it. You'll need a sturdy surface to work on, preferably a smooth one. Spread a handful of flour on the surface and pour the dough out, scraping out all the bits that stick to the sides of the bowl. To start with, the dough will be very sticky. Roll the dough around and fold it over a few times, adding flour as you go, until it is firm enough to handle, and then begin kneading.

Here's how to do it:

1. Grab the dough with both hands at the point where it is farthest away from you and fold it toward you, in half.

2. Turn the dough counter clockwise (if you are right-handed) 90 degrees so that the fold is now pointing toward the right, rather than towards you.

3. Fold it over again just as before, turn, fold again, etc. Add flour a little at a time to the surface and to your hands to prevent sticking. The total amount of flour needed can vary a great deal depending on the weather and other factors. A general rule of thumb

is that the less flour you use, the better the bread. But the bread will need to have enough flour in it to give it ample structure. Knead the bread for as long as you can stand it--10 to 15 minutes, depending on how fast you go. If you are a counter, give it 400 strokes (this is a good time to practice mindfulness). You are endeavoring to stretch out the strands of gluten in the wheat. By stretching them and folding them over on top of themselves, you are creating a "net" to catch the gases put out by the yeast as it eats the sugars in the flour and molasses. When you are finished, the dough will still be a little sticky, but should not stick earnestly to your hands.

Rising

After the dough has been kneaded, put it back in the bowl, cover it with a damp towel to prevent it from drying out, and allow it to rise in a warm place for 50 minutes. During that time, the dough should have doubled in bulk and will be filled with the gases produced by yeast. The next thing to do is to punch down the dough, pressing out all the gases and interrupting the rising process. Simply make your hand into a fist and punch all the air out. Cover again and allow to rise an additional 40 minutes.

Punch down the dough once more, roll it out of the bowl onto a floured surface, and form it into a big ball. Cut the ball in half with a knife, and then cut each half in half, making four equal pieces. Make each piece into a ball, cover with your damp towel, and allow it to relax for about ten minutes. This would be a good time to preheat your oven to 375°.

You're going to need 4 loaf pans. Coat each pan with nonstick spray and set aside. Pick one of your four pieces, turn it up-side-down on your lightly floured surface, and roll it out with a rolling pin until it is approximately a foot long and as wide as the pan. Starting at one end, roll it up into a log and put it seam side down in the loaf pan. Repeat this process with the other three pieces of dough and allow them all to rise uncovered for 20-25 minutes. They will get larger during this time, but will not completely fill the pan. They will rise a great deal more right after you put them in the oven. Try poking one gently with a finger. If the dough springs quickly back, it's not ready; if the indentation is preserved with only a little springback, then it's ready to be baked.

Baking

You'll want to give your oven plenty of time to preheat. Consistent temperature is important. Carefully place the loaves in the middle of the oven (a sudden jar can cause them to fall), close the door, and then resist the temptation to peek at them later. After about 30 minutes, rotate them in the oven so that the end of each loaf that was toward the back is now toward the front. They should be done in 40-45 minutes. You will know they are done when the bottom and sides are well browned and the loaf sounds hollow when you thump it with your finger.

The rising times given above are fairly flexible, but a suggestion is to follow them exactly the first few times until you get a feel for the process. It's possible to skip the second (40 minute) rise if you are short of time, but the quality will suffer a little. Whole grain bread requires a lot of time to work to achieve a moist and delicate consistency. The final (20-25 minutes) rise cannot be shortened or you will end up with very dense bread.

Bread making is an art form. Every batch is different, responding to a variety of factors such as the temperature, humidity, type and quality of the flour, etc. But once you get the hang of it, you can count on producing excellent bread every time.

The Bread Sequence at a Glance

1. Mix the sponge. Allow it to work for 1 hour.
2. Mix in remaining ingredients and knead well. Allow to rise 50 minutes.
3. Punch down the dough. Allow to rise again for 40 minutes.
4. Cut the dough into 4 pieces and form into balls. Allow to rise for 10 minutes.
5. Form into loaves. Preheat oven to 375°. Allow to rise 20-25 minutes.
6. Bake for 45 minutes, rotating the loaves once in the oven after 30 minutes.

Some Yeast Bread Variations

For all of the variations, mix the sponge as in the basic recipe. When it comes time to mix the dough and knead, these variations can be tried:

Nut or Seed Bread: add 2 cups walnuts, pecans, sunflower seeds, sesame seeds, etc.

Millet Bread: add 3 cups of uncooked millet

Oat Bread: add 3 cups of uncooked oats

Sunflower-millet Bread: add 1 1/2 cups millet and 1 1/2 cups of sunflower seeds

Potato Bread: add 3-4 cups of mashed potatoes (at room temperature). This makes a very yummy bread.

Oat Bran Bread: add 3 cups oat bran, grated peel from 4 oranges, 2 Tbs. coriander, 3/4 tsp. ginger, 3/4 tsp. cinnamon, 1/4 tsp. cloves, and 1 cup golden raisins (optional)

Rye-Oat Bread: add 3 cups rolled oats and substitute 3 cups of rye flour for wholewheat flour

Swedish Rye: add grated peel of 4 oranges, 1 Tbs anise seed, 1 Tbs caraway seed, and substitute 3-4 cups rye flour for wholewheat flour

Tomato Bread: substitute warm tomato juice for all or part of the water

Sweet Potato Bread: add 3-4 cups mashed sweet potatoes

Winter Squash Bread: add 3-4 cups mashed butternut, acorn or other winter squash

Just about any cooked grain can be added (2 cups or less per recipe): rice, oatmeal, polenta, etc. When adding cooked grains, however, you will need to add more flour as well because of the increased moisture content. The same is true of potato or sweet potato bread; the added moisture calls for added flour. Experiment and come up with your own combinations. If you are adding a lot to your bread, you may want to consider making 5 loaves out of it instead of 4.

BREAD IS GOOD. I LIKE HOMEMADE BREAD WITH ANYTHING.

Cinnamon Buns

Now that you know how to make yeasted breads, here's something fun for you to try. They require a little bit of effort, but they're well worth it.

Sponge:
1 cup warm water
1 Tbs. Yeast
2 Tbs. molasses
1 egg
1 1/2 cups wholewheat flour

To knead:
1 tsp. salt
1 Tbs. oil
2 to 2 1/2 cups sifted flour (white, wholewheat, or a combo)

Filling: maple syrup, cinnamon, walnuts or pecans, raisins

1. Preheat oven to 375°. Proceed as with any yeasted bread.
2. Allow dough to rise for one hour after kneading. Punch it down, knead it together, then roll it into a rectangle about ten inches wide. The dough should be thin. You may need to stop a couple of times and allow it to relax before it will stretch all the way out.
3. Dribble the top with a small amount of maple syrup and spread it out over the surface.

4. Sprinkle with cinnamon, half a cup or more raisins, one cup chopped walnuts or pecans.

5. Carefully roll the dough into a log. Pinch the seams together with a little water. Slice the log cross-ways into one-inch sections, and then arrange the slices on a tray sprayed with nonstick spray so that they are not quite touching.

6. Allow the rolls to rise for about 20 minutes, and then bake for 20 minutes, or until browned on top.

Makes about 24 buns.

Let the Ingredients Do the Talking

Let's face it. Cooking for two hundred without ever using recipes served one thing and one thing only: egocentric karmic conditioning.

One summer, as one of the weekend cooks at a renowned craft school, I wanted the meals to be the finest art work on the property. Not for the sake of the food, mind you. Not for the pure enjoyment of cooking, or for the love of the people I was serving. About this I am clear. I wanted these meals to serve as a reflection of Me. I wanted people to walk out of the dining hall making mental notes of what creative and interesting dishes were served. And, of course, it was truly icing on the cake if someone approached me with the question, "What *did* you put in the icing on that cake? Was that a touch of lime? It was fabulous!"

It wasn't until I moved to the Monastery that I considered the arrogance of that approach towards cooking. And again, let's face it, towards life. Here we follow the recipes exactly. I'll never forget the first time I worked in the Monastery kitchen and was asked to cook by the book. Black Bean Chili. You've all had it here, right? It's perfect. It's perfect because it is what it is. Straight up. Nothing prissy, fluffy, or overly anything about it. It's Black Bean Chili.

My ego had a conniption fit when I read the recipe. I had never followed someone else's cooking instructions before. My ego wanted to add ingredients, make it fancy, complicated, "special." In the world of egocentric karmic conditioning, life on its own isn't special; what ego brings to it *makes* it special. Spiritual practice has allowed me to see through this lie.

Real cooking is about getting out of the way. It's about letting the ingredients do the talking. I learned this when I toasted cumin seeds for the first time in the Monastery kitchen. I will never forget the way the warm fragrance filled the room, and how suddenly it seemed obvious that cumin does not need the assistance of an ego to be brilliant or special. It was clear that the ingredients themselves, not merely the cumin but all of them, *were* the magic.

All ego is, is the thing that wants to claim the mystery. Fortunately, with practice, the choice that becomes available is the choice of stepping aside and simply allowing life to be the magical and wondrous creation that it is all on its
own, with no help from Me.

--from a monk

Main Dishes

Here we are at the heart of the matter. As people contemplate the transition to a vegetarian diet, they are often sidetracked by the fantasy of a lifetime of boring food. In the pages that follow, you will see that there is a whole lot more to vegetarianism than spaghetti with marinara sauce. Many of the dishes in this section will satisfy even the most invested meat-eater; it's hard to imagine that anyone sitting down before a plateful of tofu loaf and gravy, or black-eyed peas and cornbread (provided that they are actually willing to experience the food) will find anything to complain about. Nobody will go away hungry, either. We work hard and eat heartily here, and these entrees provide the fuel for our vigorous lifestyle.

What in the world are you going to serve with these things? Most of the recipes that follow will include serving suggestions, but, perhaps, a few words about meal planning would be helpful.

Generally our main meal, which we eat in the middle of the day, follows this pattern:

--The first thing we consider is what sort of grain we will have. The grain will somewhat determine the direction the remainder of the meal will take, and we like to mix things up a lot. The most popular grains by far are rice and pasta, but we also enjoy couscous (a Middle Eastern type of pasta), quinoa (a delicious and

extremely nutritious grain from South America), bulger wheat, millet, spelt (in the form of bread), and corn (in the form of cornbread and polenta). Or, if we don't have a grain, we'll have potatoes, sweet potatoes, or yams, though we will often serve bread with these--for example, biscuits or cornbread with yams.

--Next we take a look at what our main protein source will be. This is where the recipes in this section come in. The protein in our diet, other than that which is found in the grains and some of the vegetables, generally comes from legumes (i.e. beans and peas) and tofu (also a legume, technically, since it is made from soybeans), and from dairy products. All sorts of variety is possible, from stews to casseroles; from Chinese stir-frys to dishes that imitate the food that most of us were brought up on, like tofu burgers or spaghetti and "meatballs." Usually, the main dish is the center of the meal, but this is not always the case. Last summer, for example, when we had loads of fresh produce coming in daily from the garden, the focus turned towards the enormous salads that we had and the heaping plates of sliced cucumbers and tomatoes, and we played down the other things--just some rice and plain beans or simple baked tofu to go with it.

--We have a vegetable or two, usually including something green.

--At lunch we have dessert.

The idea, from our point of view, is to eat in a way that provides abundantly for the body, that includes an awareness of our impact on the world around us and so nourishes the spirit as well, and that is thoroughly enjoyable. We allow simplicity to be our guide as much as possible, and we cook in a way, we hope, that honors our food. Whether you are cooking for a crowd as we do, or just for yourself, if your eye is on what will most take care of the people involved in all their aspects, the food will seem to create itself, with you as the grateful witness of it.

Tofu Pot Pie with Dumplings

Another of the many delicious recipes that Christa, our yoga teacher, has brought to us over the years, and another of the cook's favorites. The dumplings are optional; it's easier, but not as much fun, just to make biscuits and serve them on the side. With the dumplings, this is a stew; without them it's more of a soup. You might want to leave yourself a little extra time for this one.

1 cup butternut squash, peeled and chopped

1/2 of a large head of cauliflower (or 3/4 of a small one), in big chunks.

1/2 pound tofu, cut into cubes

3/4 cup carrots, diced small

3/4 cup celery, diced

1/4 cup peas, frozen

3/4 cup red potatoes, diced small

1 1/2 cups red onions, chopped small

1 Tbs. ume plum vinegar

1/2 Tbs. garlic granules

1/2 tsp. thyme

1/2 tsp. rosemary

1/4 tsp. white pepper

1/4 tsp. salt

1/4 tsp. coarse black pepper

1 Tbs. tamari/soy sauce

1/2 Tbs. white miso

1 Tbs. tahini

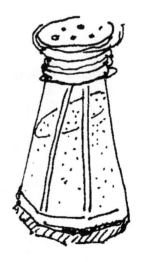

2 1/2 and 1 3/4 cups water
1/2 cube veggie bouillon
1 batch biscuit dough (page 72).

1. Cook cauliflower until mushy. In a big soup pot sauté onions, garlic, and spices in stock or water. Add the squash, carrots, potatoes and two and a half cups water. This is the beginning of the stew.
2. Boil the tofu cubes separately in one tablespoon of tamari and 1 3/4 cups water for one to two minutes.
3. In a food processor, blend cauliflower, tahini, miso and some of the water from cooking the tofu. Add this mixture to the vegetable stew along with the cooked tofu cubes. When almost done, add celery, peas and plum vinegar. Taste for flavor.
4. Mix up the biscuit dough and roll it out about one-half inch thick. Cut the dough into one-inch squares and drop the squares on top of the stew. Cover and cook at a low simmer for 20 minutes, turning the dumplings over after 10 minutes. Any leftover dough can be made into biscuits to serve on the side.

Serves four.

p.s. Ume plum vinegar can be found at most natural food stores.

Spaghetti Sauce

This is a very old Monastery recipe, originating from the Italian aunt of one of the first monks here (she called it "Nanny's Sauce"). We can only hope nobody told Nanny about soy sauce and tofu being added to her old family recipe. But, tofu or no tofu, this is the real thing.

1 medium onion, chopped

6 cloves garlic, minced

1/4 cup parsley, minced

dash salt

dash pepper

2 cups mushrooms, chopped

1 pound tofu--frozen, thawed, squeezed dry, and coarsely crumbled

1 28 oz. can tomatoes, chopped or pureed

1 15 oz. can tomato sauce

1 6 oz. can tomato paste

3 tomato paste cans of water

1 bay leaf

3 Tbs. soy sauce

2 tsp. basil

1 tsp. oregano

1 tsp. thyme

1. In a heavy skillet or pot (cast iron works well), sauté the onions and garlic in a little water. When onions are soft, add parsley, salt, pepper, mushrooms, and tofu, and mix well.
2. Add other ingredients; bring to a boil, and simmer, uncovered, for one-half to one hour. For a thicker sauce, simmer longer. Adjust seasonings as needed. If sauce is a bit tart, add one to two teaspoons brown sugar.

Serves up to ten.

Meatballs

These are sure to please even the most reluctant vegetarian. To use in Spaghetti Sauce (previous page), simply omit the tofu and add the meatballs when the sauce has finished cooking. This recipe will make enough meatballs to feed six to eight people.

1 pound tofu, drained and mashed
1/2 cup rolled oats
1/2 cup wheat germ
1/2 cup chopped onion
1 1/2 Tbs. chopped parsley
2 Tbs. soy sauce
1/2 tsp. salt

1/2 tsp. basil
1/2 tsp. oregano
1/2 tsp. garlic powder
1/3 cup toasted chopped walnuts
2 eggs
Chunky Tomato Sauce x 2

1. Preheat oven to 375°.
2. Combine all ingredients except the eggs and and tomato sauce and mix well.
3. Beat the eggs, then stir them in the tofu mixture.
4. Knead the mixture well, then form 1-inch balls and place them on a sprayed cookie sheet.
5. Bake for 30 minutes.
6. Prepare the tomato sauce, then add the meatballs when the sauce is done cooking. After that, stir the meatballs and sauce as little as possible to prevent the meatballs from coming apart.

Makes about 25 meatballs.

Chunky Tomato Sauce

This recipe makes a thick sauce that is excellent to use in casserole dishes such as lasagna, manicotti, and polenta with soysage (Phil's dish-- see "Soysage" in the Main Dish section). The other tomato sauce is thinner and better to serve on its own as an entree, with spaghetti or another pasta.

2 onions, chopped
3 cloves garlic, minced
1 medium bell pepper, diced
2 tsp. basil
1 tsp. oregano
1 tsp. thyme
1 1/2 tsp. salt

1 28 oz. can diced tomatoes
1 6 oz. can tomato paste
1/2 cup fresh minced parsley
1/4 tsp. black pepper
1 tsp. brown sugar

1. Sauté onions, garlic, bell pepper, and herbs in a bit of water until the onions are very soft.
2. Add tomatoes, tomato paste, salt, brown sugar, and black pepper. Bring to a boil, then lower heat and simmer, partially covered, for 20 to 30 minutes. Stir in the parsley. The sauce is now ready to be used in lasagna, manicotti, or any other Italian casserole.

Serves six to eight.

Bountiful Lasagna

12 lasagna noodles, uncooked

3 cups fat-free ricotta or cottage cheese

3/4 pound low-fat mozzarella cheese, grated

3/4 cup fat-free Parmesan cheese, grated

Sauce

2/3 cup onion, chopped

2 cloves garlic, minced

2 cups carrots, grated

3 cups mushrooms, sliced

3 15 oz. cans tomato sauce

3 10 oz. boxes frozen spinach (or 30 oz. fresh spinach or chard)

2 tsp. dried and crushed oregano

1. In a large skillet, sauté the onion and garlic in a little water until soft. Add the carrots, mushrooms, tomato sauce, spinach, and oregano. Heat thoroughly.

2. Preheat oven to 375°. Spread a thin layer of sauce in a large, deep casserole dish or a 9" x 18" pan, then layer one-half of the noodles, ricotta cheese, sauce, and grated cheese. Repeat, ending with the cheese. Sprinkle with grated Parmesan cheese.

3. Bake covered for 30 minutes and uncovered for 10 to 15 minutes, or until hot and bubbly.

Serves eight to ten.

Manicotti or Stuffed Shells

It's hard to imagine serving this without a salad, crusty bread, and chocolate cake. It's just what we always do.

1 box manicotti (14 pieces), or large shells
Filling:
1 3/4 cups fat-free ricotta (1 container, 15 oz.)
2 cups grated low-fat mozzarella
1/4 cup fat-free Parmesan
1/4 tsp. black pepper
1/8 tsp. nutmeg
1 egg
1/4 cup fat-free milk (or more)
1 bunch fresh spinach, chopped, or 1 10 oz. box frozen chopped spinach
Sauce:
Two batches Chunky Tomato Sauce (page 103)

1. Cook the pasta according to directions on the package. Drain and separate the pieces so they won't stick together.
2. Preheat the oven to 350°. Cook the spinach with a little water in a skillet, and drain it when it is done. Combine the filling ingredients, adding enough milk so that the cheese can be stuffed into the pasta.
3. Put a little bit of the tomato sauce on the bottom of a large casserole dish (10" x 16"). Stuff the manicotti or shells and arrange them in the pan. Pour the remaining sauce over the top. Cover with foil and bake for 40 minutes or more.

Serves about nine (1 1/2 manicotti shells per person).

Tofu Manicotti or Stuffed Shells

1 pound mashed tofu

1 clove garlic, pressed

1 tsp. salt

1/4 tsp. pepper

1 egg

1 bunch fresh spinach or 1 10-oz. box frozen spinach, cooked and well drained.

1. Combine all the ingredients.
2. Follow directions for Manicotti (previous page) substituting this filling for the more traditional one.

Serves 9.

Pasta with Creamy Tofu
(adapted from <u>Peaceful Palate</u>)

Fettuccini is the preferred type of pasta to use for this dish, but any small shape (shells, corkscrews, etc.) will work fine. We enjoy it with a spinach salad and brownies or some other chocolate dessert.

12 oz. pasta

1 onion, chopped

1/2 bell pepper, diced

1 clove garlic, minced

3 cups mushrooms, sliced

1 Tbs. parsley, finely chopped

3 Tbs. Flour

1 1/2 cups soymilk

1 tsp. salt

1/4 tsp. pepper

1/4 tsp. thyme

1/2 pound firm tofu, crumbled

1 cup green peas

1. Sauté the onion in some water until tender, then add the pepper, mushrooms, and garlic. Cover and cook until the mushrooms are well done, about six to seven minutes.
2. Whisk together the flour and the soymilk, and then add to the mushroom mixture and cook until slightly thickened.
3. Stir in remaining ingredients and heat thoroughly.
4. Meanwhile, bring a large pot of water to a boil and cook the pasta until just tender.
5. Serve the sauce over the pasta.

Serves six.

Enchilada Casserole

Your Mexican friends never need to know that you put tofu in your enchiladas.

1 pound tofu

1 small onion, chopped

3 cloves garlic, minced

1 16 oz. can diced tomatoes

1 tsp. salt

1 tsp. cumin (to taste)

1 4-oz. can chopped green chili peppers

1 20 oz. can enchilada sauce

2 cups cooked kidney beans (or one 16 oz. can), mashed

1 egg, beaten

10 oz. or more low-fat grated cheese

1 tsp. chili powder (to taste)

12 corn tortillas

1. Preheat your oven to 350°. Press the tofu (see the How To section).
2. Sauté the onion and garlic in a bit of water until the onion is tender. Add the tomatoes, half the salt, the cumin, chili peppers, and the enchilada sauce, and simmer for ten minutes or more.
3. Mash the tofu and the kidney beans together. Add the egg, the cheese, and the salt, and mix well.
4. Spoon a little of the sauce you have made into the bottom of a 9"x16" baking pan. Dip each of the tortillas in turn in the sauce to

soften them, drop a large spoonful of the filling into the center of each one, and roll the tortilla around the filling. Arrange these enchiladas seam-side down in the baking pan.

5. Pour the remaining sauce on top and sprinkle generously with cheese. Bake for thirty minutes and serve with rice and/or tortilla chips.

Serves eight to ten.

Black Bean and Spinach Burritos

One of our most popular Mexican dishes. You have a choice: you could make up the burritos and serve them ready to eat, or you might serve the tortillas and the filling separately with lots of fixings and let people build their own.

2 cups dry black beans
1 onion, chopped
4 cloves garlic, peeled and minced
1 red bell pepper, in mouth-sized strips
1 28-ounce can diced tomatoes
1 tsp. cumin
1 tsp. chili powder
1 tsp. salt
1 large bunch fresh spinach, washed and stemmed (or 1 ten-ounce package frozen chopped spinach, thawed and drained).
1 cup fresh or frozen corn
Flour tortillas
Grated low-fat cheese
Salsa

1. Sort, soak, and cook the beans (see the How To section for specifics).
2. In a large skillet, sauté the onion and garlic in a bit of water until soft, then add the tomatoes, pepper, spinach, corn, and the seasonings, and cook for ten more minutes.

3. Mash about half the beans, and add them to the vegetables with enough of the bean cooking liquid to give the mixture a soupy consistency.

4. To make the burritos, drop a couple of large spoonfuls of the bean mixture into the center of each tortilla and add grated low-fat cheese and salsa if desired. Fold up the bottom to make a pouch to catch the filling, then roll each tortilla around the beans and fixings. The burritos could either be served as they are, or you could arrange them seam-side down on a baking sheet, drizzle them with enchilada sauce and sprinkle them with cheese, and put them in the oven at 350° until the cheese melts on top.

Serves 8.

Chilaquiles Casserole

Our buddy Christa made this up for us as an interesting way to use up leftover beans and vegetables and old tortillas. We'll often have a casserole like this one on Sundays, when there is not much time to cook because of the schedule. We prepare it a day ahead and bake it when we're ready.

1 28 oz. can enchilada sauce
6 corn tortillas, torn into pieces (tortilla chips are ok)
3 cups leftovers (such as beans, chili, burritos, onions, garlic)
2 oz. canned green chilies, diced
1/4 pound low-fat mozzarella cheese, grated
1/2 cup fat-free sour cream

1. Preheat oven to 375°.
2. Spray a casserole dish with nonstick coating. Layer ingredients in the following order: sauce, tortilla pieces, leftovers, chilies, cheese, sour cream.
3. Repeat the layers, and then add more sauce and cheese. If there is extra sauce and tortillas, put them on top.
4. Bake for one hour.

Serves four to five.

Mjeddrah

(from <u>The Peaceful Palate</u>)

Mjeddrah (moo-jed'-rah) is a Middle Eastern lentil-rice dish that is served topped with a vegetable salad, and dressed with a lemon vinaigrette. We will often serve wedges of pita bread on the side.

2 large onions, coarsely chopped

3/4 cup brown rice, uncooked

1 1/2 cups lentils (uncooked), rinsed

4 cups water

1 1/2 tsp. salt

1. Cook the onions in a little bit of water in a large pot until the onions are soft. Add rice and continue cooking over medium heat for three minutes.
2. Stir in lentils and water. Bring to a simmer, then cover and cook 40 to 50 minutes, until the rice and lentils are tender. Add salt.

Salad

2 large tomatoes

1 cucumber

2 to 3 green onions

1 green or red bell pepper (or 1/2 of each)

1 stalk celery

Optional: lettuce, avocados, sprouts, radishes...

1. Dice all ingredients and toss with Lemon-Thyme Dressing (page 62).

Serves six to eight.

Curried Mushrooms and Chickpeas
(adapted from _The Peaceful Palate_)

It's handy to be able to borrow ideas from Asia and India, where vegetarianism has been a part of the culture for centuries. This is one of several Indian dishes that we regularly enjoy.

1/2 cup water

2 large onions, chopped

1 1/2 Tbs. whole cumin

1 1/2 pounds mushrooms, sliced

1 28-oz. can whole tomatoes, chopped with juice

2 cups cooked garbanzo beans (or 1 15 oz. can, drained)

1 tsp. turmeric

1 tsp. coriander

1/2 tsp. ginger

1 tsp. salt

1. Sauté the onions in the water for two to three minutes, then add cumin seed and mushrooms. Continue cooking over medium heat until onions are soft and mushrooms are browned.

2. Chop the tomatoes with their juice (easily done in a blender) and add to the onions along with the garbanzo beans and spices. Cook 20 to 30 minutes, or longer if time allows, until the mushrooms are tender and most of the liquid has disappeared. Add salt to taste. Serve with rice, yogurt, a chutney, and any steamed vegetable.

Serves eight.

Yellow Dal

A "dal" is an Indian bean dish. Serve this one with rice, yogurt, a chutney, and greens for an Asian feast.

1 cup yellow split peas
3 cups water
1 onion, chopped
2 tsp. curry powder
1/2 tsp. turmeric
1/2 tsp. chili powder
1/4 tsp. ground cumin
3 cloves garlic, crushed
1 tsp. fresh ginger root, finely minced
1 16-ounce can diced tomatoes and juice
1/2 pound green peas, fresh or frozen
1/2 tsp. salt

1. Cook the split peas in the water at a simmer for an hour or more, or until they have disintegrated.
2. Sauté the onion in a bit of water until tender. Add all remaining ingredients except the yellow and the green peas, bring to a boil, and simmer for ten minutes.
3. Add the yellow peas, the green peas, and additional water if needed (the consistency should resemble a stew). Cook for five more minutes, and serve.

Serves six.

Rajma (Curried Red Kidney Beans)
(from <u>Bean Banquets</u>)

This dish is good with rice, yogurt, a chutney, and steamed greens.

1/2 pound dried red kidney beans

1 onion, chopped

1 Tbs. finely chopped fresh ginger

1 large clove garlic, mashed

1 two-inch stick cinnamon

2 whole cloves

2 whole cardamom pods

1 tsp. turmeric

1 Tbs. ground coriander

1/2 tsp. ground cumin

4 peeled and diced ripe tomatoes

1 tsp. salt

a few sprigs fresh, chopped coriander leaves, if available

1. Cook the beans (see the How To section).
2. In a large saucepan, sauté the onion, ginger, garlic, cinnamon stick, cloves, and cardamom pods in some water until onion is soft and just beginning to brown.
3. Add ground coriander, turmeric, and cumin and continue to cook and stir for five minutes.
4. Add tomato and cook and stir until mixture loses most of its moisture and becomes a paste.
5. Pour beans and bean broth over the paste and stir. Bring to a boil, lower heat, and let simmer for a few minutes to allow flavors to blend.
6. Shortly before serving, add fresh coriander leaves, if available.

Serves three or four.

Vegetable and Tofu Stir-Fry

Often, the stir-fry is one of the first things people will attempt as they begin to venture into the scary and dangerous world of vegetarian cooking. It's easy and fun, and there is no exact way to go about it. Every stir-fry is different, and you can experiment to see what best appeals to you. We have included a few guidelines below to help get you started.

First, we like to spread everything out that we think we might like to have in our stir-fry, and see what tickles our fancy. Some of our favorite stir-fry vegetables are carrots, cabbage, peppers, snow peas, broccoli, cauliflower, summer squashes, and greens, and we always throw in some tofu cubes as well. We figure that a third of a pound of tofu, a half pound of vegetables, and plenty of rice will feed a hungry monk. When you are choosing what you would like to have in your stir-fry, remember the appeal of a variety of colors and textures. For example, imagine a mixture of broccoli, carrot, and red pepper; or red cabbage, cauliflower, and snow peas. Nuts and seeds may also be a fine addition.

The next step is to cut up all the vegetables. Have fun with it; they can be as artful as you like. How about little carrot matchsticks instead of plain circles, or long, thin pepper slices instead of squares? You'll want to leave everything fairly large so that each vegetable will remain distinct. Once the cooking process begins, everything tends to happen in a big hurry, so you'll want to prepare everything ahead and arrange it strategically around the stove before you get started.

If you have a wok, use that; if not, a cast iron skillet is the next best thing. Whatever you have, heat it over a high flame and wait to add any food until it's good and hot. We do not use oil, so our stir-frys are not technically "fried." Instead, we use a little no-stick spray and water, if needed, with very pleasing results. When the pan is hot, spray it and then add some vegetables. The trick when stir-frying is to cook things at a high temperature very quickly, beginning with those vegetables which will require the most time in the wok and then proceeding with those which will require less, and so on, so that everything will finish at the same time. We usually start with an onion, and, when it is almost done, we begin adding longer-cooking vegetables, such as cauliflower, cabbage, winter squash, carrots, and celery. Vegetables such as broccoli, summer squash, peppers, and mushrooms cook more quickly and can be added to the wok after a little bit, when the time is right (a little practice will teach you how to recognize this moment). Greens prefer to be added at the end of the cooking time; spinach, in particular, will cook almost instantly upon contact with the other hot vegetables. The tofu can be handled in a couple of ways: it can be cooked separately in the same manner as the vegetables and added towards the end, or it can simply be thrown in with the longer-cooking vegetables. It's a nice touch to marinade the tofu first, if you are so inclined (see the How To section).

The stir-fry may be seasoned in a variety of ways. The simplest is to add garlic and fresh ginger with the shorter-cooking vegetables, and soy sauce to taste. If you don't mind a little added complexity, try the sauce that follows. You might try western herbs instead of the Oriental flavors, especially fresh basil (and salt and pepper). Your stir-fry will be at its very best right when it has finished cooking. Rice or Oriental noodles are the natural accompaniments, but other grains, such as quinoa or bulgur, can be good as well.

Orange Stir-Fry Sauce

Pineapple chunks are a delicious addition to stir-fry dishes, so if you like, you could open up a can and cook the fruit with the vegetables and use the juice in this sauce.

3/4 cup orange or pineapple juice
1/4 cup soy sauce
1 1/2 Tbs. grated fresh ginger
3 cloves garlic, minced
2 Tbs. cornstarch

1. Combine first four ingredients.
2. Place cornstarch in a bowl and whisk liquid mixture into it.
3. When you are ready to cook the sauce, whisk it together again and pour it over the vegetables in the wok. Stir everything constantly from the bottom until the sauce comes to a boil and thickens, coating the vegetables and tofu.

Each sauce will serve four.

Fried Rice

This is an excellent way to use up leftover rice. You can make a one-dish meal out of this recipe with the addition of cubed tofu.

8 cups cooked basmati (or other) rice
1 onion, chopped fine
2 Tbs. minced ginger
6 cloves garlic, minced
1 red pepper, in thin strips
1 pound peas, or a handful of snow peas
other vegetables: mushrooms, cabbage, etc.
nonstick spray plus 2 tsp. oil
1/2 cup soy sauce

1. Sauté the onion, garlic, and ginger in the nonstick spray and oil until translucent (around five minutes).
2. Add the pepper, peas, and any other vegetables and continue cooking until everything is done.
3. Add the rice and soy sauce and fry until heated through.

Serves eight to ten.

Marinated Tofu

This recipe goes way back to the first of our Monastery Cooks. There's no telling how many times we've served it. We recommend white basmati rice, steamed broccoli, and carrot cake to go with it.

2 pounds tofu, pressed
3 Tbs. soy sauce
3 Tbs. vinegar, rice or cider
1 clove garlic, minced or pressed
2 Tbs. toasted sesame seeds
1 tsp. ginger, grated
3 green onions, minced

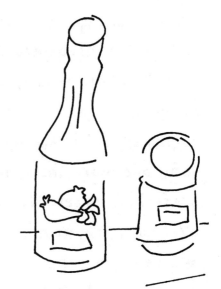

1. Press tofu for 30 minutes.
2. Combine the soy sauce and vinegar in a bowl. Mince garlic, grate ginger and add to the liquids. Toast sesame seeds and add to the marinade.
3. Cut the pressed tofu into approximately half-inch cubes. Toss the tofu with the marinade. Add the green onions and toss well. Marinate for a couple of hours, or overnight, in the refrigerator.
4. Bake for 30 minutes at 325°, covered with foil, and then ten minutes uncovered.

Serves four.

Five Varieties of Baked Tofu

An easy and wonderful way to prepare tofu is to bake it. Here are five different marinades that you might use to flavor the tofu, and each one may be served with the baked tofu as a sauce. These go well with rice and steamed vegetables. Each of the following recipes will produce enough marinade to cover one pound of tofu, which will serve 2-3 at the Monastery and 3-4 just about any place else.

Baking tofu is easy. Step one is to slice your block of tofu into five or six slabs and lay the slices out in a flat-bottomed pan or storage container. Next, mix up one of the marinades below, pour it over the tofu, and marinate in the refrigerator for at least two hours, preferably longer. We usually prepare the tofu and marinade in the evening and marinate all night. Preheat your oven to 400°. When you are ready, pull the tofu slices out of the marinade and place them on a sprayed baking sheet. Bake them for a half hour or more, turning them over once. The longer you bake them, the firmer they become. In the meantime, heat up the marinade. The first four marinades below will need to be thickened with cornstarch (instructions for this will follow); the final one will not. When the tofu has finished baking, arrange it on a platter and pour the hot sauce on top to serve.

Garlic and Ginger Marinade

1/2 cup soy sauce
4 cloves garlic, minced
4 tsp. grated fresh ginger
2 Tbs. toasted sesame seeds
2 Tbs. rice vinegar (or cider)
2 tsp. sugar
1/4 cup water

Five-Spice Marinade

(Five-spice powder is found in the Oriental section of supermarkets.)

1/2 cup soy sauce

4 cloves garlic, minced

2 Tbs. rice vinegar

2 tsp. sugar

1/2 tsp. 5-spice powder

1/4 cup water

Sweet and Sour Marinade

3 green onions, minced

1 tsp. minced fresh garlic

1/2 cup vegetable broth (made from bouillon or broth powder)

2 Tbs. ketchup

1/4 cup water

1 Tbs. soy sauce

1 Tbs. rice vinegar

1 Tbs. sugar

1/4 tsp. chili powder

Ginger-Orange Marinade

3/4 cup orange juice

2 cloves garlic, minced

1 Tbs. minced ginger

1/4 cup soy sauce

1/2 tsp. salt

1/4 tsp. pepper

1 Tbs. sugar

1 green onion, minced

To turn the above marinades into sauces by thickening them with cornstarch, whisk 2 teaspoons of cornstarch per cup of liquid into the marinade, and heat over a medium flame, stirring constantly. The sauce will thicken as it comes to a boil (see "Thickening Liquids" in the How To section). The marinade below will be thick enough to serve as a sauce without this step. This recipe will marinate 2 pounds of tofu.

Miso Sauce

1 cup mirin

1 cup applejuice

4 Tbs. miso (any type)

1/3 cup chopped, toasted walnuts

1 Tbs. rice vinegar

2 small cloves garlic, minced

1 tsp. salt

Tofu Stew

2 pounds tofu

3 Tbs. soy sauce

2 large red potatoes, peeled, cubed

3 carrots, peeled and sliced

2 onions, cut into chunks

2 stalks celery, sliced

1/2 pound frozen peas

5 cloves garlic

5 to 6 cups water

1 large bouillon cube

1/2 cup + 1 Tbs. whole-wheat flour

2 bay leaves

1/4 tsp. pepper

3/4 tsp. basil

3/4 tsp. thyme

1/2 tsp. sage

1/2 tsp. turmeric

1/2 tsp. chili powder

1 tsp. salt

1. Cut tofu into half-inch cubes and freeze overnight. When you are ready to make the stew, bring a large pot of water to boil, drop in the frozen tofu cubes, and allow them to thaw in the hot water.

2. Drain the tofu and rinse with cold water. Pat tofu cubes dry with a towel and sauté them with the soy sauce in a skillet sprayed with nonstick spray.

3. Place the 5 cups of water, the bouillon cube, bay leaves, and garlic in a soup pot. Bring to a boil, add all the vegetables except for the peas, and simmer until everything is tender.

4. While the vegetables are cooking, lightly toast the flour in a dry, heavy-bottomed iron pot until it has lightly browned. Allow the flour to cool a little, then whisk in the cooking liquid. Bring to a simmer, stirring constantly, over medium heat. It will thicken as it comes to a boil; when it has, turn the heat down to very low, add the seasonings, and cook for 5 more minutes.

5. Add this gravy and the peas to the vegetables and simmer a little while longer, adding more water if needed. Serve with a heaping plateful of biscuits and a salad or mixed steamed vegetables.

Serves six or more.

Tofu Burgers
(from The Peaceful Palate)

The best meatless burgers they have ever had, many say. Don't forget the oven fries.

1 pound firm tofu, drained and mashed
1/2 cup rolled oats
1/2 cup wheat germ
1/2 cup onion, chopped in small pieces
1 1/2 Tbs. parsley, finely chopped
2 Tbs. soy sauce
1/4 tsp. salt
1/2 tsp. each, basil, oregano, garlic powder
3 Tbs. toasted, chopped almonds

1. Preheat oven to 350°.
2. Mix all ingredients and knead for about one minute, or until mixture holds together.
3. Shape into bun-sized patties, and bake on a baking sheet coated with nonstick spray for 25 to 30 minutes.

Serves four to five.

Tofu Croquettes
(adapted from <u>The Peaceful Palate</u>)

A very old favorite. You can tell when a monk served as the Head Cook by how he or she makes the croquettes: the newer folks roll them into balls, while the old-timers tend to make them into little pyramids. We pretty much always serve croquettes with mashed potatoes and gravy, a steamed vegetable, and Pumpkin Pie or Lemon Meringue Pie for dessert.

2 cups water
1/4 tsp. salt
1 cup brown rice, uncooked
14 oz. firm tofu, mashed
1/4 cup toasted tahini
1/2 small onion, finely chopped
2 Tbs. soy sauce
1/2 cup finely chopped parsley

1. Bring water to a boil. Add salt and brown rice.
2. Allow water to return to a simmer, then cover and cook until rice is tender (about 50 minutes). Allow to cool.
3. Preheat oven to 350°. Mix remaining ingredients with the cooked rice.
4. Form into balls, one to two inches in diameter.
5. Place on a baking sheet sprayed with nonstick spray and bake until browned, about 25 minutes.

Makes about 25 croquettes.

Tofu Loaf

This recipe overcomes the difficulty confronting every new vegetarian: what in the world am I going to have for Thanksgiving? We feast grandly every year, and then we meditate for four days (we call it the "Gratitude Sesshin"). Along with the Tofu Loaf, we have mashed potatoes and gravy, yams or baked winter squash, peas and carrots, cranberry sauce, and not one but two pies--pumpkin and pecan. It is very, very difficult to feel deprived under those circumstances.

1 cup chopped onion	2 Tbs. chopped parsley
1 cup diced green pepper	1/4 cup soy sauce
1 cup diced mushrooms	1 tsp. salt
1 1/4 pounds extra-firm tofu	3/4 tsp. basil
1 cup wheat germ	3/4 tsp. oregano
1 cup rolled oats	3/4 tsp. garlic powder
1/3 cup walnuts, chopped	2 eggs, beaten lightly

1. Preheat oven to 350°. Sauté onion, peppers, and mushrooms in a tiny bit of water until well cooked.
2. In a large bowl mash the tofu, then combine with all the other ingredients (including the vegetables and eggs) and mix well. It helps to knead the mixture with your hands to make it stick together.
3. Press into a loaf pan sprayed generously with nonstick spray and bake for 45 minutes to one hour. To serve, slice the loaf while it's still in the pan and then invert it onto a plate and cover the top with gravy or ketchup.

Serves eight.

Tofu with Tartar Sauce

Do you remember those fish sticks they had at the school cafeteria? Thank heavens those days are over. We offer this as a saner and far tastier version of that American...classic.

1 pound tofu (press for 30 min.)

Marinade:

2 tsp. salt   1/2 tsp. pepper
1 cup water

Dredge:

1/4 cup cornmeal   1/8 tsp. garlic powder
1 Tbs. nutritional yeast   1/8 tsp. curry powder
2 Tbs. wheat germ   1/8 tsp. thyme

Tartar Sauce:

1 cup low-fat mayonnaise   3/4 tsp. curry powder
1/3 cup pickle relish   1/4 tsp. salt
1 1/2 Tbs. cider vinegar   1/8 tsp. onion powder

1. Cut the pressed tofu into 1/2" x 1/2" x 4" strips and marinate them in the water and salt and pepper for at least two hours.
2. Preheat the oven to 350°.

3. Mix together the cornmeal, yeast, wheat germ, garlic powder, curry powder and thyme.

4. Drain the tofu and dredge each strip in this cornmeal mixture. Place on a lightly sprayed baking sheet.

5. To make the tartar sauce, combine the mayonnaise, relish, vinegar, 3/4 teaspoon curry powder, salt, and onion powder. Mix thoroughly.

6. Bake the coated tofu for 30 minutes (or longer). Arrange on a platter and serve with the tartar sauce.

Serves two to three.

Chili Beans

(adapted from _The Peaceful Palate_)

3 cups dry pinto beans

8 to 9 cups water

4 cloves garlic, minced

1 tsp. cumin

2 onions, chopped

2 bell peppers, diced

1 28 oz. can tomato sauce

2 cups corn, fresh or frozen

1 1/2 tsp. chili powder

1 tsp. salt

1. Wash the beans thoroughly, then soak overnight.
2. Discard the soaking water. Place the beans in a large kettle with fresh water and cook with the garlic and cumin until tender, about one and a half hours.
3. Sauté the onion and bell pepper in water until the onion is soft. Add to the cooked beans, along with the tomato sauce, corn, and chili powder. Simmer at least 30 minutes.

Serves eight.

Corn Pone
(adapted from <u>The Peaceful Palate</u>)

A bean pie with a cornmeal crust--it's an old Southern tradition. If you don't have leftover chili beans to use, any will do if they are mixed with plenty of tomato sauce, some chili powder, and a little ground cumin.

6 cups chili beans (page 131)
2 cups soymilk
2 Tbs. vinegar
2 1/2 cups cornmeal
2 tsp. baking soda
1/2 tsp. salt
2 Tbs. oil

1. Preheat oven to 400°. Combine the soymilk and vinegar and let stand five minutes or more.
2. Heat the beans until they are very hot, then pour them into a 9" x 12" baking dish.
3. Mix the dry ingredients in a large bowl, and add the soymilk mixture and the oil.
4. Stir together just to mix, then pour over the hot beans, and bake until the cornbread is set and golden brown, about 30 minutes.

Serves eight to ten.

Soysage

We don't know where this recipe came from, but it's a great one. Use Soysage for making Hash, as a pizza topping, spread over polenta (see next page), or as it is with gravy.

3 pounds tofu, frozen and thawed, and squeezed dry
1 cup wholewheat flour
1 1/2 tsp. pepper
1 1/2 tsp. sage
1 1/2 tsp. thyme
1 1/2 tsp. ground savory
1 1/2 tsp. coriander
3/4 tsp. mace
1/3 cup soy sauce

1. Preheat the oven to 375°. Mix all the ingredients. Knead to make it all stick together.
2. Bake on a cookie sheet sprayed with nonstick spray for 30 to 45 minutes. Scrape pan occasionally to prevent sticking.

Serves five.

Phil's Dish

A very popular way to serve Soysage is in a casserole with polenta and tomato sauce (sometimes known as "Phil's Dish" after a monk who lived here).

To make the casserole:

1. Cook some polenta (page 4).
2. Spread it in the bottom of a deep baking dish.
3. Cover the polenta with a lot of Chunky Tomato Sauce (p. 103).
4. Layer the sauce with the Soysage.
5. Cover the dish, and bake at 350° for 1/2 hour or more.

Hash

This is a very hearty dish. Serve it with a big batch of Gravy (page 154) and some sort of steamed vegetable, especially greens or a mixture of peas and carrots.

1 recipe Soysage (with 3 pounds tofu) (page 133)
3 pounds potatoes
2 onions, coarsely chopped
8 cloves garlic, minced
2 green bell peppers, cut into 1 1/2 inch strips
2 tsp. salt
1/2 tsp. pepper
2 tsp. olive oil

1. Make the Soysage.
2. Peel the potatoes and cut them into half-inch cubes. Steam them until just tender (eight to ten minutes).
3. Spray an iron skillet with nonstick spray, add the oil, and sauté the onions and garlic until the onions are soft. Add the peppers and continue cooking until tender. Add potatoes, salt, and pepper and cook three to five minutes.
4. Mix in the Soysage and serve hot, with the gravy on the side.

Serves eight.

Black-Eyed Peas

This dish became popular at a time when over half the monks here were from North Carolina, and it has stuck even with all the Yankees who are around these days. In the South it is said that if you eat black-eyed peas on New Year's Day, you will have good luck all year, and this has certainly been the case with us. We like our peas with cornbread, beets and greens, and either a cobbler or pumpkin pie for dessert.

1 pound black-eyed peas
1 onion, chopped
6 cloves garlic, minced
1 green pepper, chopped
1 28 oz. can diced tomatoes
1 tsp. salt
2 Tbs. (or more) soy sauce
1/2 tsp. thyme
1/4 tsp. pepper

1. Cook peas, saving liquid.
2. Sauté onions and garlic in water until tender.
3. Add pepper and tomatoes and cook ten minutes.
4. Combine peas, vegetables, seasonings, and as much of the reserved cooking liquid as needed for a stew-like consistency. Simmer five minutes, and serve.

Serves eight.

Macaroni and Cheese

This is about as American as it gets. Prepare this dish as written for a fifties-style Macaroni and Cheese, or add chopped tomatoes and chopped spinach or other vegetables for a more up to date version. Breadcrumbs can easily be made in a food processor.

8 ounces macaroni
2 eggs
1 cup low-fat cheese, grated
1 cup cottage cheese
1 1/3 cups milk
1/4 tsp. paprika
bread crumbs

1. Cook the macaroni until just tender and drain.
2. Beat the eggs together in a large bowl. Add the macaroni and all the remaining ingredients except the breadcrumbs and mix well.
3. Pour into an 8x8-inch casserole dish that has been sprayed with nonstick spray, top with the breadcrumbs and bake at 350° for 40 to 50 minutes, or until set. We enjoy this dish with plain soup beans (i.e. red beans, white beans, kidney beans, etc.) and a salad.

Serves 6-8.

Cheri's Pizza

If you're like me, you're going to buy a crust at the store. However, this pizza would be better for you, and would doubtless taste better, with a Monastery crust. The quantities of the ingredients can vary depending on your taste. These are layers. Make them as thin or as thick as you like.

one pizza crust
red onion, thinly sliced
low-fat feta cheese
low-fat mozzarella
avocado
tomato

1. Preheat oven to 450°.
2. In any order and in any amount you choose, layer the prepared crust with onion rings, feta, and grated mozzarella.
3. Bake until crust is brown and cheese is bubbly--12 minutes maybe?
4. While the pizza is cooking, slice your tomato, and schmoosh your avocado in a bowl.
5. When the pizza is done, spread the avocado over the top, gently, as if you are frosting a cake.
6. Arrange your tomato slices on the top.
7. Enjoy.

Serves one (if you're like me).

Pizza

1 1/4 cups hot water (120° to 130°)

1/4 oz. package regular yeast

1 tsp. brown sugar

1 tsp. salt

3 Tbs. toasted wheat germ

1 1/2 cups unbleached white flour

1 1/4 cups wholewheat flour

1/4 cup protein powder

additional flour for kneading

Chunky Tomato Sauce (page 103) or canned tomato sauce

toppings of your choice

shredded low-fat mozzarella cheese

1. Preheat oven to 375°. Pour water into medium bowl; sprinkle in yeast. Stir with wire whisk to dissolve quickly. Add salt, brown sugar and wheat germ.

2. Add white flour, wholewheat flour, and protein powder. With a sturdy wooden or stainless steel spoon, stir until dough forms mass and leaves the sides of bowl.

3. Knead dough for about five minutes (kneading instructions, page 89) adding flour as needed to keep dough from sticking. Cover with a damp cloth and let rise for at least 15 minutes and up to one hour (the longer, the better).

4. While dough rises, prepare a batch of Chunky Tomato Sauce and whatever toppings you would like. Mushrooms, onions, black olives,

tofu or Soysage (recipe page 133) carrots, eggplant, and squash are all popular at the Monastery.

5. Coat one 12x18-inch baking pan (or equivalent circular pan) with nonstick spray. Punch all the air out of the dough, form it into a ball, and roll it out until it is large enough to cover the pan. It may be that the dough is not willing to spread so far at first. In this case, you can roll it out, allow it to relax for five minutes, roll it out some more, allow it to relax, and so on until it is large enough.

6. Place the rolled-out dough in the pan and press it out to the edges, forming a lip around the outside with your fingers to hold in the tomato sauce and toppings.

7. Ladle some tomato sauce on top of the pizza dough. Spread your toppings over the sauce and cover with a generous amount of cheese.

8. Bake for 25 to 30 minutes, until the crust is browned on the bottom.

Serves 6 or 7.

The Blind Monk and the Carrots

I was working in the kitchen one day along with the cook and our blind monk. The monk was given an assignment that required the use of a cutting board. There are two large ones kept out on the center table in the kitchen. When not in use, one is put face down on the other one. The monk knows her way around the kitchen and is not shy when going about her duties there (at least, that is my projection from my rather tenuous nature in that hotbed of spiritual practice). She felt around the edges for the little feet in the corners of the cutting board, confirmed it was face down, and proceeded to hoist it up to shoulder height and turn it over.

What she didn't know was that a large pile of carrots had been grated on the upside down cutting board. The cook had a look of shocked disbelief as the carrots cascaded off the righted board. As luck would have it, they fell very neatly onto the cutting board that was face up underneath, a major stroke of luck or divine providence. The monk very nonchalantly went about her chopping, never knowing what had transpired. The contrast between her calm demeanor throughout the episode and the cook's look of horror struck me as quite humorous in that rather sober (my projection) environment. It was refreshing that nothing had to be said about it. Life just went on.

--from a monk

141

Lines from the Kitchen

In every moment
we are consciously or unconsciously creating ourselves,
each other, and the world around us.
Make it something great.

If you don't limit what you believe is possible, you will find that there are no limits
on you as to the beauty and impact of what you can choose to create and be.

Life isn't happening to you; you are happening to it.
Life is the experience of creating experience.
★★★★

As far as I can remember, I have been fascinated by bridges.
Literal bridges joining pieces of land separated by water.
Bridges in songs, joining two separate melodies.
Ambassadors.
Translators.
A gymnast daring to connect an arch, a curl, a stretch with the air.
An artist communicating an enigmatic vision into a stroke, a color, a vibration,
a pitch, a texture.

And, so, I bring this admiration to cooking.
Exploring semiotics. Exploring myself. Looking at what is.
Being willing to be with this moment, with these ingredients.
Sometimes, often, it is not all this poetic.
But in those moments of willingness, of 1-2-3-4...
I bridge this level of beingness, and translate energy from the food, into the food.
Translating this reality into one that will be ingested and absorbed into the blood
stream, into the lifestream.

Form is not different from emptiness,
Emptiness is not different from form.

It is quite a miracle, actually.
Washing kale from the garden. Its deep greens and purples. Colors I didn't know
existed in my urban-reality.
Then cutting. Admiring the shapes. How did this come from a seed?
Placing the bounty in a steamer.
Then on the dining room table.
Then on my plate.
And I chew.
Knowing that I do not know.

I sometimes cry when I visit the garden. Its overflowing of chlorophyll-green. Its
willingness to trust the earth and air and sun. I marvel at photosynthesis. These
plants aren't trying to grow. They just do.
I remind the seedlings (clearly reminding myself) that it is safe to trust the earth.
It is safe to reach out their roots from beyond their previous potted-lives, into
the abundance. The overflowing earth. The rich warmth of the sun, and the cooling
of the night air. It is safe.
★★★

I often pour my intention as an extra ingredient into whatever I am cooking.
Sometimes it's acceptance bread.
or willingness cookies.
or gratefulness cake.
I think it works.
★★★

Dessert is my favorite.
When I came to the Monastery for the first time on a TINW retreat,
and there were cupcakes on the table,
I knew I was in the right place.

--From a monk

Tofu Dave

We eat a heck of a lot of tofu. In fact, the handful of us monks eat more tofu than the entire town of Angels Camp altogether. I know this because on shopping day we could wipe out every morsel that both of the supermarkets have on their shelves, and there would still not be enough.

We have to call the supermarket on Mondays to order it by the case. I think the most I've bought so far at one time is sixty pounds--it filled half a shopping cart. We buy so much tofu that, towards the beginning of my two-year shopping stint, I earned the nickname "Tofu Dave" at the main supermarket. Every Thursday it was the same: I'd find the produce guy bent over a pile of beets or carrots or something, and when he saw me he'd say, "Tofu Dave! What's shakin'? You need some tofu?" I resisted it a little at first, but I sort of liked it after I got used to it, and then I ended up introducing myself that way. I had the same conversation with him every week when I called in on Mondays: "Tofu Dave here." "How many?" "Four please." "You got it." I have a soft spot in my heart for precision and consistency, and I grew to be quite fond of the produce guy. One time, when the Monastery needed to contact me during my weekly shopping adventure, they had me paged over the loudspeakers: "Tofu Dave, line one please. Tofu Dave, line one."

So a couple of years of Thursday shopping expeditions passed by, another monk took over the job, and I moved on to other things. Then, during a retreat, it was decided that we'd give the cook a break, and I'd do the shopping trip that week. Over a year had passed, but at the grocery store, incredibly, it was all the same. The same rowdy stockers were there cracking the same jokes, the same bad music was playing over the speakers, and when I found the produce guy bent over a pile of lettuce he said, "Tofu Dave! What's shakin'? You need some tofu?" Later on I wheeled my five cart-loads up to the check-out stand as before, and I noticed that both the check-out lady and the bagger were new--must have been hired since my shopping days, I thought to myself. The checkout lady worked her way through a couple of carts, and when she got to the produce she said, "Hmm. That's an awful lot of tofu." "Sure is," I said agreeably. Then the bagger jumped in and said, "Hell,

144

that's nothin'. We used to have this guy come in here named Tofu Dave, and he'd buy so much tofu..."

It was nice to be remembered.

--from Tofu Dave, a monk

Nothing to Do with Cooking

Of the many hours I've spent cooking at the Monastery, this is my favorite kitchen--not cooking--story, and it has absolutely nothing to do with food. I was the snack cook on a typical summer afternoon. "HOT!" is the most descriptive word to use. I was in an out-of-the-present-moment mind-state. "What am I doing here? Nothing I do seems to work, and everything just gets worse and worse." Despair. So I started fantasizing: There's a little house tucked into the hills by the ocean. The dune grass is swaying in the light breeze. I can smell the fresh sea air as I sit in my garden full of larkspur and black-eyed susan and iris. (Meanwhile, I can smell the cookies burning back at the Monastery.) The sun is shining, and there are trails that go for miles beginning right outside my back door. And a dog. A loving dog, sitting by my side. A dog. Yes, a dog. I want a dog. This last piece of the fantasy had a slightly different quality to it. It felt as if a very young part of me had been waiting for a long time to be heard, and there was finally a little space that was open to receiving her. And she wanted a dog. Those words kept coming over and over again. I want a dog. Yes, a dog. A dog. I want a dog. It didn't have the quality of endless desire to it (like popping burnt cookie after burnt cookie into my mouth). It had a quality of sweetness that opened my heart a little bit. I went on with my day, feeling lighter, and didn't give it another thought.

Three days later, I was working in the kitchen for the afternoon, and a dog found her way to the porch right outside the dining hall doors. I went immediately to investigate. She was the skinniest ninny you've ever seen, covered in dirt, and looking like she had just had puppies. I asked the retreatant, who was standing nearby (oops, broke a guideline), "Is she yours?" He said, "No, I walked up that hill over there, and she followed me back. Maybe she belongs to the monk who lives up there." I'm the monk who lives up there! Holy Cow! It occurred to me in that moment that I might have a dog. Wow! I didn't tell anybody, but I somehow ended up being the one to feed her, and she started coming home with me at night. A few weeks later, we had a kids' retreat, and she received her official name-- Samantha Wild Crazy--better known as Sam to her loved ones (which includes you, since one of her amazing qualities is that she seems to love all people unconditionally). I aspire to be like Sam.

It was about a month later that "The Traveler" in me got a bit nervous and wasn't sure she was ready for such a stable, year-round reminder of her heart. But The Traveler and I decided that traveling wasn't much to give up for the sweetest peanut in the universe (we can all own that projection). So now I have a full-time, furry teacher, thanks to the creative juices of the Monastery kitchen.

Faith is what this experience has brought into my life and a great curiosity about how this kind of thing can happen. I've practiced with this a lot and have found that, if there is a place inside me that is genuinely open to receiving, life can't seem to help but meet itself. I'm convinced that the transformation I'm seeking through spiritual practice is nothing more than allowing myself to receive wholeheartedly, with every ounce of my being, all that is being offered. ("Nothing" is not the best word to use because it feels like an outrageous challenge.) As I consider this, colors look more vibrant and everything feels a little more whole. Riding right underneath this is a current of energy that I label "fear." One of the monks was saying in group the other night that he keeps hoping to find a place where there is absolutely no suffering, where it's just completely gone, and that he hasn't found it and just keeps practicing. I experienced "no suffering" while he was saying that, and I bet he did too, right before he spoke. It's subtle, but there was a small place inside me that was open to receiving that place of no suffering, and I went there for just a moment. It feels like the same experience that happened to me in the kitchen that day. I was thinking, "What would it be like if I allowed myself to receive in that way moment to moment to moment to moment?" Holy Smokes! Life feels different at just the thought of it. Pretty amazing stuff I've experienced in the Monastery kitchen.

So, now I've told my favorite cooking story that has absolutely nothing to do with cooking. I have to wonder what it would be like if I allowed myself to receive all the amazingly delicious food there is in my life--and to receive *making* amazingly delicious food. YUM! Many thanks to all the cooks.

--from a monk

Side Dishes

This section highlights those recipes that often do not get as much credit as the rest. How unfair, don't you think, that because they are perhaps not so impressive as a main dish, or not as subtle as a salad or as glamorous as a dessert, we should overlook the role these dishes play in our pleasure at the table? What would tofu loaf be without gravy, for example? How could we have Thanksgiving without apple-cranberry sauce? The other day when, for whatever reason, we had no oven fries with our tofu burgers, it was like somebody had died. How can we not have oven fries with our tofu burgers? We always have oven fries with our tofu burgers! These are the dishes that round out our meals; they represent that little extra bit of attention that help us all feel welcome and cared for.

Often, people who are learning to cook are frustrated by the lack of information about the simple foods they most love. Try to find a basic mashed potato recipe--it's not easy. If you've been making mashed potatoes since you were two, it might not occur to you that somebody might need help with this, but if you're taking up cooking at thirty-five and have never even boiled a spud, a dish of mashed potatoes may seem as mysterious as the Dharma. Hopefully, here and in other places in this book, we have to some extent bridged that gap. It's never too late to learn to cook. Even if you already know how to cook, it's not too late. Wonderfully, there isn't any place to get to with it. The joy is in the learning; as we learn we grow, and as we grow, we ourselves become, you might say, the thing that is cooked. If we are fortunate, we will be very well cooked and as much esteemed and appreciated by those who understand cooking as, for example, Yams with Cranberries and Apples or Tuscan Beans.

Tuscan Beans

1 pound dried small white beans
3 large cloves garlic
5 leaves fresh sage

1 Tbs. extra virgin olive oil
salt and pepper to taste

1. Sort through beans and remove any small stones or shriveled beans. Rinse and place beans in a bowl, adding enough water to cover by at least two inches. Let soak at least four hours or overnight.

2. Preheat oven to 300°.

3. Drain the beans, rinse again and drain. Place the beans in a flameproof casserole and add enough water to cover by one inch. Add the garlic, sage, and olive oil, and bring to a slight simmer over low heat.

4. Once the beans are simmering, remove from the stove and place them in the oven. Cover and cook 45 minutes to one hour or more, or until the beans are very tender. Check occasionally to see that the beans remain covered with water.

5. When the beans are tender, add salt and pepper to taste and return to the oven for another five minutes. Just before serving, drain some of the juice from the beans and adjust taste if needed with olive oil, salt and pepper. Serve warm or at room temperature. We enjoy this dish as an accompaniment to Italian dishes such as spaghetti and meatballs or lasagna.

Makes about four cups.

Refried Beans

(adapted from <u>The Peaceful Palate</u>)

This is one of our favorite ways to eat beans. Serve these with brown rice, tortillas, and burrito fixings--grated cheese, sour cream, chopped tomatoes, chopped avacado, a big bowl of lettuce, and salsa.

1 1/2 cups dry pinto beans
4 cups water
2 cloves garlic, minced
1 tsp. cumin

1 onion, chopped
2 cloves garlic, minced
1 15-ounce can diced tomatoes with their juice
1 small can Anaheim chilies
1-2 tsp. salt

1. Cook the beans thoroughly with the garlic and the cumin (see the How To section).
2. Sauté the onion and garlic in a little water until the onion is completely cooked. Stir in the tomatoes, chilies and salt, then add the beans a spoonful at a time, mashing them as you go. Add as much of the bean cooking water as you need to reach a soupy but not sloppy consistency. The beans will thicken considerably as they cool.

Serves 6 to 8.

Oven Roasted Beets

6 beets, cut in 1/4 inch slices
1/2 Tbs. olive oil
salt to taste
pepper to taste

1. Preheat oven to 400°.
2. Clean and slice beets.
3. Put beets in a bowl and toss with barely enough oil to coat them. Add salt and pepper.
4. Place on a baking sheet that has been sprayed with nonstick spray, turning every twenty minutes, until edges are crispy and beets are done.

Variations:

This same recipe works well with a mixture of carrots, onions, and mushrooms instead of the beets. For an even more interesting flavor, add red potatoes and dried rosemary.

Serves four to five.

Scrambled Tofu-Potato

Like scrambled eggs, only better.

1 onion, chopped
4 cloves garlic, minced
4 cups sliced mushrooms
6 green onions
2 pounds tofu, drained and mashed
1 pound red or white potatoes, peeled and diced
Nonstick spray plus 2 tsp. oil
2 tsp. salt
1/2 tsp. pepper
1 Tbs. curry powder

1. Steam the potatoes until just tender, about eight minutes.
2. Heat an iron skillet over a medium flame. Spray with nonstick spray. Add the oil, onion, garlic, and mushrooms, and sauté until the onions are cooked, about eight minutes.
3. Add all remaining ingredients and sauté about five more minutes. It may be necessary to add a little water to prevent sticking.

Serves six to eight.

Mashed Potatoes

Sometimes people will come to spend time with us at the Monastery never having been exposed to a week of vegetarian cooking before. They wonder how they will survive on peanut butter and crackers for that long. Imagine their relief when the table rolls out with a huge mound of mashed potatoes on it and a pot of steaming gravy on the side.

3 pounds red potatoes, peeled, and cut into chunks
1/4 cup sour cream
1/4 cup lowfat mayonnaise
1 tsp. salt
1/4 tsp. pepper
milk as needed

1. Steam the potatoes until done (about ten minutes).
2. Mash with the remaining ingredients, adding milk as needed.

(To make a non-dairy version, omit the sour cream and mayo and use tofu mayo and soymilk instead, or just soymilk.)

Serves six.

P.s. We do not buy peanut butter, and there are a number of monks who would willingly trade in the potatoes any day.

Gravy

What would mashed potatoes be without gravy? People tend to think they are saying goodbye to gravy forever when they commit to a vegetarian diet, but this is not the case at all. We think the following recipe produces an excellent gravy without the use of animal products and with no added fat. See the How To section under "thickening liquids" for more information about the techniques called for below.

Our favorite gravy:

1/3 of an onion, chopped small
3 cups (or less) sliced mushrooms
2 Tbs. wholewheat pastry flour
1 cup unsweetened soymilk (preferably)
1/4-1/2 tsp. salt
1/4 tsp. thyme
1/8 tsp. pepper

1. The first step is to toast the flour over medium heat in a dry, thick-bottomed pan or skillet (cast iron is ideal). This will eliminate the raw flavor of the flour and give the gravy a nice toasted taste and color. To toast the flour, first heat up the pan, then add the flour and stir it constantly with a spatula or flat-edged wooden spoon until it lightly browns. This will not take long--two to five minutes, depending on how hot the skillet is. It is easy for the flour to burn during this process; if it does you'll have to start over, as this will impart an unpleasant flavor to the gravy. Any variation in the ratio between the flour and the soymilk will affect the

consistency of the gravy, so it is important to measure both carefully. When the flour has browned, remove the skillet from the heat and continue stirring until the flour is no longer being cooked.

2. Allow the flour to cool for at least five minutes, and then whisk the soymilk and the flour together until the flour is dissolved.

3. Meanwhile, sauté the onions in another thick-bottomed pan until they are well cooked. Add the mushrooms and continue cooking until they are done, as well.

4. Whisk the flour/soymilk mixture together again to make sure the flour is well incorporated, and then pour it into the pot with the onions and mushrooms, scraping the sides of the pan to make sure you've got every bit.

5. Bring it all to a boil, stirring constantly to prevent burning. The gravy will thicken as it comes to a boil.

6. Reduce the heat to very low, add the seasonings, and cook, stirring often, for five minutes. If the gravy is not served right away it will thicken more as it cools, in which case you can simply add more soymilk to get the consistency you desire.

Some variations:

Soymilk is not the only liquid you can use in this recipe to make good gravy. We also love to use the water that is left over from cooking beans, especially kidney beans. To make bean stock gravy just substitute the stock for the soymilk, and add a pinch of marjoram along with the other seasonings. You could also use vegetable broth (made from bouillon and water), the water left over from cooking potatoes, or cow's milk. You could also experiment with other seasonings, in particular garlic, mace, sage, savory, and soy sauce in small amounts.

Scalloped Potatoes

2 pounds red or white potatoes, peeled, washed, and thickly sliced
1/2 pound cheese, grated (or part cheese, part cottage cheese)
1/2 onion, chopped
2 eggs
1 cup milk
2 Tbs. flour
2 tsp. salt
3/4 tsp. pepper
1/4 tsp. thyme
a pinch of nutmeg
grated Parmesan cheese
bread crumbs

1. Preheat oven to 350°. Coat an 8" x 8" casserole dish with nonstick spray.
2. Steam the potatoes until just tender.
3. Arrange a layer of potatoes in the bottom of the dish, sprinkle them with a little of the salt and pepper, some of the onion, and cover with a light layer of cheese. Continue making layers in this way until all of these ingredients are used.
4. Beat together the eggs, milk, and flour. Add any remaining salt and pepper, the nutmeg, and the thyme. Pour this mixture over the potatoes (it should come just to the top), sprinkle with Parmesan and bread crumbs, and bake for 45 to 50 minutes until browned.

Serves six.

Mushrooms Sautéed in Broth

This recipe is an excellent topping for baked potatoes.

1 cup water

1 vegetable bouillon cube

1 pound mushrooms, sliced

1. Bring water to a boil and add bouillon cube. Stir until dissolved.
2. Add mushrooms and sauté gently until soft.

Serves six to eight.

Yams with Cranberries and Apples
(adapted from <u>The Peaceful Palate</u>)

This is a popular dish with us on Thanksgiving. We'll also serve it in the evening, sometimes with yogurt or cottage cheese for a light meal.

4 large yams, peeled
1 large green apple, peeled and diced
1 cup raw cranberries
1/2 cup raisins
2 Tbs. sugar or other sweetener
1/2 cup orange juice

1. Preheat the oven to 350°. Cut peeled yams into one-inch chunks and place in a large baking dish.
2. Top with diced apple, cranberries and raisins. Sprinkle with sugar or other sweetener, then pour orange juice over all.
3. Cover and bake for 1 hour and 15 minutes, or until yams are tender when pierced with a fork.

Serves six to eight.

Applesauce

This is where apples go when they get old. We like applesauce just about any time, but especially at breakfast.

6 apples, cored and cut into very small chunks
3/4 cup water
1/4 cup maple syrup or sugar
1 tsp. cinnamon
2 tsp. lemon juice
a pinch of salt

1. Put the apples in a pan with the water, bring to a boil, cover, and steam apples until very tender (ten to fifteen minutes).
2. Add remaining ingredients and mash. Chill.

(To make apple-cranberry sauce, substitute a package of cranberries for three of the apples. You'll need to add 1/4 cup more sugar and enough extra water to give it the consistency you like.)

Serves six.

Apricot Chutney

1 cup dried apricots, chopped
2 cups boiling water
1/2 cup raisins
5 cloves garlic, minced
1 tsp. grated fresh ginger root
1/2 cup red wine vinegar
3/4 cup sugar
a hearty pinch of salt

1. Plump the apricots by pouring the boiling water over them and allowing them to stand for ten minutes or more.
2. Add remaining ingredients and bring to a boil. Reduce the heat and cook at a gentle, bubbly simmer until the chutney has thickened (this may take an hour or more). You'll need to watch it carefully towards the end and stir when needed to see that it doesn't burn.
3. Allow to cool before serving. This chutney is good both at room temperature and chilled.

Makes about two cups.

Spiced Tomato Chutney

This is one of our favorite chutneys. We'll serve it along with yogurt beside any number of Indian dishes (see the Main Dish section for a couple of samples).

3 cups peeled tomatoes (fresh or canned)
1/2 cup vinegar (white or red wine)
1/2 cup sugar
6 cloves garlic, crushed
1 Tbs. fresh ginger root, minced
1/4 tsp. salt
1/4 tsp. cinnamon
1/4 cup raisins

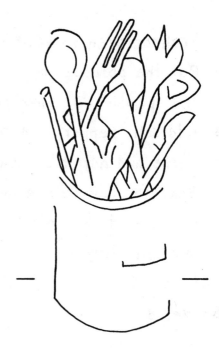

1. Combine all ingredients in a medium saucepan and bring to a boil.
2. Reduce to a gentle simmer and cook until the chutney has thickened. This may take anywhere from an hour to two hours, depending upon how juicy your tomatoes are. Take care to stir occasionally, especially towards the end, to prevent burning.
3. Serve at room temperature, or chilled.

Makes two cups, or more.

Oven Fries

4 pounds red potatoes
1 1/2 Tbs. olive oil
1 tsp. salt
1/2 tsp. pepper
1 Tbs. or more dried rosemary

1. Preheat oven to 400°. Spray a large baking pan with nonstick spray.
2. Cut the potatoes into fat french-fry chunks, place in a large bowl and sprinkle with olive oil. Combine well.
3. Add salt, pepper, and rosemary and mix well.
4. Taste and adjust seasonings as needed.
5. Bake for one to one and a quarter hours or more, depending on the size of the potato chunks. Stir every 15 minutes or so to prevent sticking.

Serves 8.

Practice Like Your Shirt Is On Fire

In the Monastery kitchen the spices are kept on a section of counter just to the right of our large gas range. We use many spices here, which makes the spice rack and surrounding area a bit full, and, if you ask me, chaotic. When I was cook assistant, I dreaded being handed a recipe which called for a long list of spices. The same humiliating routine happened again and again: I'd look for the spice I needed and not find it. "We must be out," I'd say to myself. "It's not here, nowhere to be found." Next step, hand a note to the cook: "We are out of oregano." The cook would graciously accept my note, walk over to the spices, grab the oregano and hand it to me. This was a regular occurrence.

One day I was given the recipe for pumpkin pie. "Ok, nutmeg. No problem. Let's go find the nutmeg. Here we go." (Can you sense the energy building?) I head to the spice rack and look. No nutmeg. "Okay, I can do this. I am going to bring all of my attention to the spices. I will become one with the spices. The nutmeg will reveal itself to me." I wedge myself in between the stove and the counter and lean in, determined. I am a monk with a cause. I will succeed. I'm even a little excited at this point. I'm rounding a new bend in my practice. I'm training myself to really attend. Think of the possibilities! I'll be unstoppable.

Next thing I know I hear a squeak from the cook who starts hitting my back with a potholder, putting out my sweatshirt, aflame from the burner next to me. Before I could react, the fire was out and the cook had returned to her soup. I just stood there, unhurt but humbled. So much for paying attention.

Incidentally, when I was made cook, the first thing I did was arrange those spices the "right way," the "logical" way. Then, no one would have to run into their karma like I did.

--from a monk

Hungry Ghosts

During a *There Is Nothing Wrong With You* retreat, a drawing of "hungry ghosts"* was posted on the bulletin board in the dining hall.

Later in the week one of the other retreatants mentioned in a group discussion how he had taken the drawing to mean he shouldn't eat too much while at the Monastery. His literal interpretation of this concept led him to cut back on how much of the delicious food he would serve himself, thinking the ideal was to become a hungry ghost.

He was able to laugh when he realized it was a figurative concept, and that he could start eating normally again.

--from a retreatant

*Hungry ghosts are symbolic creatures with tiny mouths, skinny necks, and huge bellies. No matter how much they eat they can never be satisfied. They symbolize the futility of trying to placate ego's incessant desires.

About Rice, Sort of

Every night after dinner the monks whirl around the kitchen in a ballet of cleaning and organizing. During my first retreat, I received a general orientation about how to assist in meal clean-up, but when confronted with the sight of the experienced monks washing, wiping, and storing, I became intimidated. I made it my goal to get into the kitchen early every night for meal clean-up. That way, I could be sure to station myself as either the dishwasher, rinser, or dryer, as these were jobs that I understood how to do. This worked well until one night when I took a little too long enjoying my dinner. By the time I got into the kitchen for meal clean-up, every task I felt comfortable with was taken. I thought, "Well, great. Now what?"

I watched as monks took plastic containers from the closet, filled them with leftovers, and labeled them. I thought, "Well, here's something I think I can do." I saw a small amount of brown rice in one of the huge serving bowls. I picked out a container that I thought the rice would fit, spooned in the rice, and noticed that it filled only half of the container. But I applied a label and turned away, looking for something else to do.

A minute later I turned back around and saw a monk pick up the container I had just set down. Would he notice that I had only filled it half way? Was that going to be a problem after all? Why was he looking at my container, dang it? Didn't he know I was new to this clean-up business? Didn't he know I was trying my best? WHY WAS HE LOOKING AT MY CONTAINER?

Then he emptied the rice into a smaller container. Instantly I felt my cheeks flush with anger. I glared at the monk, and I pictured sending sharp daggers flying at him. I thought, "Who does he think he is? Can't he see I am doing my best? Can't he see I'm trying? He is such a #$*@¢!!! Oh, I hate everyone here!"

In my mind, he was criticizing me. In my mind, he was calling me stupid. In my mind, he was saying, "Oh, that dumb girl can't even put rice away correctly!"

In my mind. In my mind. In my mind.

It was ALL in my mind. None of it was real, but I was reacting as if it were. My heart raced. My blood boiled. I was angry. And then--well--and then something happened. Time stood still. I remember thinking, "Here is this monk I've never even said a word to, and here I am ready to punch his lights out." What was going on? How could I hate this person I didn't even know? I realized I hated him because I thought he was trying to hurt me. But was he trying to hurt me? He was just silently transferring rice from one container to another. I heard a voice in my head say, "This is what you do. You feel you're not good enough, and then you hate." I saw it for the first time. I was taking my self-hate and projecting it outward.

Tears welled up in my eyes. I escaped into one of the dormitory bathrooms, locked the door, sat on the floor, and cried.

My thoughts raced: How long had I been "protecting" myself through anger and hatred? I suspected it had been going on for a long time, and for the first time I saw what was isolating me from loving myself and others.

That was when I "got it" that I wanted to move forward in my life with spiritual practice. In my heart, I began to feel the goodness that was possible. The simple act of recognizing my pattern loosened its grasp on me. The last days of my retreat were spent connecting with more love and kindness in my heart than I had ever experienced.

One last thing: Later on I told my rice-container awakening story in a guidance appointment with a monk. At the end, as I was walking away, the monk mentioned, "Oh, and you know, it's just about space. We don't have a lot of space in the refrigerators, so we have to be very precise with the containers fitting the food." I laughed. What a silly thing for me to get upset about. What a great opportunity for spiritual practice.

--from a retreatant

166

Spreads

Traditionally, Buddhist monks do not eat after noon. They take their begging bowls around in the morning, eat whatever they are offered, and, once the middle of the day has passed, they fast until the next morning. Alas, we are a cowardly set of monks, and we love our food too well to follow such a noble example. But, in honor of our spiritual roots, we call our evening meal "snack" and try to keep things simple. Along with the soup and the bread and everything else, you will often find a spread there. Our spreads are very popular, and the ones made of tofu will often excite curiosity about this wonderful food not normally included in Western diets.

We call them "spreads" so that we have something to call them, but a lot of folks never spread them on anything. You can turn a green salad into a main dish, for example, with the addition of a generous spoonful on top, or you could just eat your spread with a spoon.

If you are inclined to experiment and create your own spreads, it is not at all hard to do. The basic tofu spread formula is very simple: to one pound of tofu, drained and mashed, add a tablespoon of lemon juice (or more), a teaspoon of salt, and whatever else you fancy. Just about any vegetable in small pieces will work, most herbs and spices, and all nuts and seeds.
The sky is the limit. If you stumble across anything that is particularly good, let us know. We'd love to have the recipe.

The Original Tofu Spread

This is the first tofu spread that we had, many years ago, and the inspiration for all the others.

1 pound tofu
1 carrot, grated
3 green onions, chopped
1/4 cup soy sauce
2 Tbs. lemon juice

1. Squeeze tofu to remove excess moisture. Mash well, then mix in remaining ingredients.
2. Chill before serving.

Serves 6.

Mock Tuna Salad

(from *The Peaceful Palate*)

Popular as a topping for baked potatoes.

1 15oz. can garbanzo beans, drained
1 stalk celery, finely chopped
1 carrot, grated (optional)
1 green onion, finely chopped
2 Tbs. mayonnaise
2 Tbs. sweet pickle relish
1/2 tsp. salt (optional)

1. Mash the garbanzo beans with a fork or potato masher. Leave some chunks.
2. Add the sliced celery, grated carrot, chopped onion, mayonnaise, and relish and mix well.

Serves 4.

Hummus

Hummus, the Middle-Eastern chickpea spread, is often people's first introduction to an alternative, vegetable-based diet. Most recipes you'll find are loaded with fat in the form of olive oil and tahini (roasted sesame-seed paste, easily found in natural food stores). This one represents a compromise.

3 cups cooked chickpeas (two 15 1/2 oz. cans, rinsed and drained)
2 cloves garlic, peeled and chopped
1 cup chopped parsley (packed)
2 green onions, chopped
2 Tbs. tahini
1/4 cup lemon juice
3/4 salt (or more)
a pinch of cumin (optional)

1. If you have a food processor, use it to mince the garlic, parsley, and onions together. If you don't, chop them all together into tiny bits.
2. Add the remaining ingredients and process it all together to make a thick paste, or, alternatively, mash the chickpeas by hand and then stir in what remains.
3. Chill until serving.

Serves 6 to 8.

Tofu Hummus

1 can chickpeas, or 2 cups cooked chickpeas
1/2 pound tofu, mashed
2 Tbs. tahini
1 cup stemmed parsley (packed)
3 Tbs. lemon juice
1/2 tsp. salt
2 cloves garlic, minced

1. Process the chickpeas in a food processor or blender until smooth.
2. Add remaining ingredients and process again until smooth. Chill.

Serves 6.

Tofu "Egg" Salad

"More like egg salad than egg salad," as one retreatant put it. This is a very popular idea, and there must be a hundred recipes out there. This is the one we've grown fond of.

1 pound firm tofu, drained and crumbled
1/4 cup low-fat mayonnaise
2 Tbs. prepared mustard
1 Tbs. soy sauce
1/2 tsp. ground turmeric
3 to 4 green onions, finely chopped
1/4 cup celery, minced
2 Tbs. dill pickle relish

1. Mash the tofu.
2. Add remaining ingredients and mix well.
3. Chill until serving.

Serves 5 or 6.

Tofu-Mushroom Spread

4 cups finely chopped mushrooms
8 scallions, chopped

2 pounds tofu, mashed
1 Tbs. lemon juice
2 Tbs. soy sauce
3/4 tsp. thyme
3/4 tsp. salt

1. Sauté the mushrooms in a bit of water until soft.
2. Add the scallions and cook about two minutes more.
3. Combine the mushroom mixture with the remaining ingredients and mix well.

Serves 10.

Tofu-Spinach Spread

Very green, very yummy.

1 pound tofu
2 Tbs. lemon juice
1 clove garlic, mashed
3/4 tsp. oregano
1 tsp. salt
1/4 tsp. pepper
1 bunch spinach
1/4 cup walnuts, toasted and chopped (optional)

1. Mash the tofu and combine it in a bowl with everything except the spinach and mix well.
2. Stem and wash the spinach in two changes of water, shake or spin out excess water, and then mince it into tiny pieces.
3. Toss the spinach with the tofu mixture and chill.

Serves 6.

Tofu-Artichoke Spread

4 Tbs. lemon juice
1/2 tsp. oregano
1 tsp. basil
1/2 tsp. thyme
Lots of fresh ground pepper
3 medium cloves garlic
2 tsp. salt
2 pounds tofu
2 cans artichoke hearts, drained and chopped

1. Put lemon juice, basil, oregano, thyme, pepper, garlic, and salt in a food processor and process until the garlic is well minced. Add 1/2 pound tofu and process until smooth. Transfer to a bowl.

2. Mash the rest of the tofu with a fork or potato masher and add it and the artichokes to the above mixture. Mix well.

Serves 8 to 10.

Tofu-Avocado Spread

Next time you have Cheri over for supper, serve her miso-squash soup, biscuits, and this spread. It's sure to be a hit.

1 pound tofu, drained and mashed
2 Tbs. lemon juice
1 tsp. salt
1/2 tsp. ground cumin
4 avocados, mashed

1. Combine all ingredients and chill.

Serves 8.

Miso Walnut Spread

Ketchup? This recipe is the product of one of those moments when everything seems possible.

1 pound tofu, drained and mashed
3 Tbs. red miso
2 tsp. lemon juice
1/3 cup ketchup
1/3 cup chopped walnuts

1. Combine everything but the walnuts and mix well.
2. Add the walnuts and chill.

Serves 6.

Tofu-Basil Spread

A must in the summer when we have basil in the garden. If you don't have the vegetables to add, try it with chopped toasted walnuts.

2 pounds tofu
2 gloves garlic, peeled
2 Tbs. lemon juice
1/4 cup, or more, fresh basil (or 2 tsp. dried).
1 tsp. salt

Optional: grated zucchini, chopped tomatoes, or diced avocados

1. Combine half-pound tofu and the garlic, lemon juice, basil and salt in a food processor until mixture is smooth.
2. Mash the remaining tofu. Mix it with the blend from Step 1. Add the (optional) vegetables. Mix together well and chill.

Serves 10.

Tofu-Ginger-Sesame Spread

2 pounds tofu, drained and mashed

1/4 cup lemon juice

1 1/2 tsp. salt

1 Tbs. grated ginger

1/3 cup toasted sesame seeds

1. Mix all ingredients together well and chill.

Serves 10.

Tofu-Horseradish-Olive Spread

2 pounds tofu, drained and mashed

3 Tbs. lemon juice

1 1/2 tsp. salt

2 Tbs. prepared horseradish

1 four-ounce can sliced ripe olives

1. Combine all ingredients and chill.

Serves 10.

Tofu-Miso Spread

This is a good way to get to know miso if you are unfamiliar with that wonderful food.

2 pounds tofu, drained and mashed
1/2 cup miso (red, if possible)
1 1/2 Tbs. lemon juice
1 carrot, grated
1 garlic clove, crushed
1 zucchini, grated
1/2 green pepper, minced
1/2 small red onion, minced

1. Combine the tofu, miso and lemon juice.
2. Add the remaining ingredients. Combine well and chill.

Serves 10-12.

Tofu-Zucchini-Sunflower Spread

2 pounds tofu, drained and mashed

3 cloves garlic, peeled

2 Tbs. lemon juice

2 1/2 tsp. dried basil

2 tsp. salt

1 zucchini, grated

1/4 cup sunflower seeds, toasted

1. Put 1/4 pound of tofu, all of the garlic, lemon juice, basil, and salt in a food processor and process until smooth.
2. Place remaining tofu in a bowl and add the processed mixture, the grated zucchini, and the sunflower seeds and mix well. Chill and serve.

Serves 10-12.

White Bean Spread

2 cups cooked small white beans

2 cloves garlic, chopped

1/4 cup chopped fresh basil (or 2 tsp. dried)

2 tsp. red wine vinegar

1/4 tsp. salt

a pinch pepper

1. Combine all ingredients in a food processor. Process until smooth.
2. Chill before serving.

Serves 8.

Open-Face Breadless Fall Sandwich

I'm crazy about the food at the Monastery, except, of course, the few things I learned not to like when growing up. Combine that with no menu planning, no shopping, and relatively little cooking, and we're getting pretty close to heaven. Every once in awhile, though, there's a hankering to get creative with food. That's why Sunday evenings are the best of the best. When there are no quests, just us chickens, we have a "pickup snack." The cook leaves a list of leftovers for us to choose from, and we're on our own. Besides getting a taste of the last week's favorites, we can get as wild and crazy with food combinations as our imagination allows. Who says split pea soup, tofu "fish" sticks on a biscuit, and watermelon don't go together? Letting something other than habit guide the food choices is a lot of fun.

I've got a sandwich mentality when it comes to food preparation, so here's my personal Sunday Snack favorite when the fall apples come into season:

Core and slice a crisp apple into rings. Spread apple rings with a little spicy brown mustard. Top with several layers of very thinly sliced cheese. Lettuce is great on this "sandwich," too (if it's on the cook's list of "available foods," of course.) If you don't like how sticky the apple makes your fingers, you could slide a rice cake underneath, but I don't recommend it. I'm dying to try this with a few raisins on top, but have never seen raisins on the "available foods" list. And why not have cold mixed garden greens, with soy sauce as a side dish? Call them Chilled Asian Greens. Nab a piece of leftover chocolate cake, too, if it's not all gone.

--from a monk

Yummiest Cake Ever

I haven't lived here at the Monastery for very long, so I don't have any of those wonderful history-making stories to relate. I have had a couple of "interesting" things happen, though.

The first is the time I made a sweet and sour paste for Sweet and Sour Tofu by misreading "tablespoons" for "teaspoons" when adding the cornstarch. Oops. Really thick paste. Midway through the noon meditation period, just before lunch, it occurred to me, in a flash, what I'd done. Yet another helpful insight, a little too late.

The second is the time I was asked to bake the yummy chocolate cake we often have at Sunday lunch. It was the first time I had been in charge of this important task. Alas, after measuring, mixing, and pouring with great care, when I pulled the cakes from the oven, the edges were baked perfectly, but the middles had sunk to the thickness of a cookie. Then, when I silently took one of the cakes over to the Cook, made gassho (bowed), and showed her the mishap, she turned around and we both spontaneously burst out laughing. Although we laughed for only a brief second, it was long enough, I fear, to raise a question in the minds of several people who, just at that moment, were arriving for the Precepts Retreat: Just how silent is this silent Monastery? Incidentally, after new cakes were baked, those middles were cut out and served as leftovers; it was some of the yummiest cake I've tasted.

--from a monk

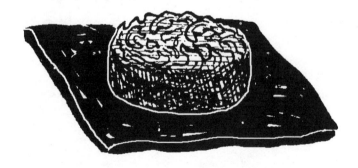

The Science Project

"I don't cook" and am rarely asked to do working meditation in the kitchen. But during a sesshin (a time when we all participate in an intense sitting schedule and observe strictest silence), we all take our turn preparing very simple meals. I was assigned the task of making the Cocoa Pudding Squares and optimistically prepared myself for tackling a "real" cooking job. At the point in this recipe where we're instructed to pour copious amounts of boiling water on <u>top</u> of the other carefully mixed ingredients, I thought, "This has got to be a mistake, this just isn't right!" Horror and disbelief almost lured this good monk into breaking silence and pointing out the grievous recipe error to anyone within earshot. Fortunately, my monastic training kicked in, along with a quarter-teaspoon of faith, and I just followed the recipe, fully expecting the results to be the most disastrous dessert on record.

Well, I'm here to tell you it works and is better magic than a sixth grade science project!

--from a monk

Designer Carafes

Making soy milk is a great exercise in paying attention. I can't tell you how many spiritual opportunities have come up whenever I've been assigned to make it here at the Monastery. After the water reaches a rolling boil, there's timing the blending in conjunction with the squeezing of the bag, and, when you've been careful enough not to let any of the mashed up okara ooze over, there's re-heating of the soy milk, making sure the bubbly surface doesn't rise up and spill out all over the range (ahem, speaking from personal experience, yes, I did "hit the gas instead of the break" so to speak).

My favorite time making it was when I put the hot soy milk into our plastic storage containers a bit too early. I poured it in, got busy with something else, and turned around just in time to see those nice containers becoming amorphous designer carafes (which we still use!). But, please, don't let my enthusiastic description of the process discourage you from making it. Straining your own soy milk lets you decide whether to sweeten or not to sweeten, and making your own is far cheaper than the store bought stuff and tastes better too.

--from a monk

Desserts

Ah, yes--dessert. As Cheri has been heard to say, "We all need a little sweetness in our lives." Folks are sometimes surprised that sweets are available here at the Monastery. Either they have brought with them an image of Zen that is austere and self-denying, or they wonder along these lines: If the Monastery's intention is to care for the monks and others who practice here at a level they are not able to accomplish for themselves, and if people come here to learn what it means to be truly taken care of (by themselves), then how can we serve something like sugar to them, as this is something that most people would agree does not nurture the body?

Here's the way we look at it: People almost invariably associate spiritual practice with deprivation, and it serves no one to support that notion. If the acceptance of the enormous challenge of a spiritual life requires that we give up all that we love and enjoy, then we will not follow that path for long because, without the space that enjoyment creates in our lives, there is not room for the heart, and where there is no heart, there is no willingness. Deprivation has nothing to do with spiritual practice; it is another name for that which desires us to suffer. Do you feel guilty when you reach for that slice of pie? If so, then we would recommend that you have another, and ask your internal judge by what authority it would shame you for the pleasure you find in it. When people begin to look closely at this issue, many recognize that they would rather die of sugar poisoning than to live for another moment with the notion that self-denial will make them good people. It never will--it will only make them feel deprived.

This is not to say there is no middle way. With the attention that we bring to our experience here, it is difficult to overlook the connection between the chocolate cake and the uncomfortable sensation in the stomach afterwards, and if a monk wishes to experiment with the possibility of saving his or her body that uneasiness, there will be support for that. We must all learn how to decide, in freedom, what we want. Dessert is not the issue; how we relate to ourselves is the issue--having it or not having it is irrelevant when compassion is there. And when you're having it, we figure, it might as well be something yummy.

Note to the 2003 edition:

Not long after this cookbook was first published, something happened here at the Monastery that has changed our relationship to dessert. It began when a woman came to train with us who struggled with a difficult sugar addiction. As we watched her wrestle very hard with her fixation, we saw how difficult it was for her to be faced with sugar three times a day at meals. Inspired by her efforts, we decided as a community to support her by eliminating refined sugars from our diet for the time that she was with us. The effect of this on her addiction, as you might expect, was profound; what we hadn't anticipated is that we would discover that we were all addicted to sugar. By the time she left us we had grown to feel so grateful for sugarless meals that we decided not to go back.

When we have guests now we serve dessert at lunch as we used to do, for all of the reasons mentioned in the original introduction to this section. We have experimented with reducing the sugar in our regular dessert recipes, and have found that in most cases the dessert is actually improved. To our delight, we have discovered that the pleasure that comes with feeding ourselves something that cares for the body is deeper and more satisfying than choices that only thrill the senses. When we are on our own these days, instead of cakes and pies we enjoy sweet salads or fruit at the end of a meal. We still very much enjoy sweet things, after all; it's just that our preferences have changed. Who needs a sugary dessert when you can delight your eyes and tummy with a great big slice of watermelon, or with a delicate citrus salad instead?

The recipes that follow reflect our changed perspective. In most, the sugar has been cut by a third to a half. In addition we have included two sugar-free desserts that we have enjoyed regularly: the baked apples and the baked pears with walnuts. You might also look to the salad section of this book to find recipes there that will work as dessert (try the carrot-beet salad, for example). If you suspect that like us you suffer from a secret (or not so secret) addiction to sugar, we hope that you will experiment as we have to find a way to satisfy both your natural love of pleasure and your body's desire to thrive, and we hope that the recipes that follow will assist you in that direction.

Baked Pears

Here is a delicious example of how less is more. Since we discovered it, this fat free, sugarless dessert has become a favorite. Something magical happens to a pear when it is baked. Why hide its unique flavor with a bunch of unhealthy ingredients? Let this be an inspiration to you to do some experimenting of your own.

Firm pears
balsamic Vinegar
toasted walnuts

1. Preheat oven to 350°.
2. Slice pears in half, remove stems and seeds, brush or drizzle with balsamic vinegar, then place face down on a sprayed cookie sheet.
3. Bake for thirty minutes to an hour, until tender. The harder the pear, the longer it will take to cook. When it's done it will be tender and the skin will become brown and wrinkled.
4. Serve face-up on a platter, drizzled with more balsamic vinegar and sprinkled with toasted walnuts. We like to serve extra vinegar and walnuts on the side.

One pear serves one person.

Baked Apples

Another fruit dessert with no fat or sugar. We hope you'll find it as delicious and satisfying as we do.

4 large, tart apples
3 to 5 pitted dates, chopped
1 tsp. cinnamon

1. Wash apples, then remove core to within 1/4 inch of bottoms. Combine dates and cinnamon, then distribute equally into centers of the apples.
2. Place in a baking dish filled with 1/4 inch of hot water and bake at 350° for 40-60 minutes.
3. Serve hot or chilled.

Serves four.

Chinese Chews

This is an old family recipe from one of our Sangha (group of people who meditate together) members. It was found in a women's magazine in the early 1900s. It is a holiday cookie, but we think it makes any day feel like a holiday. Each year, at our New Year's Retreat, we meditate into the new year, the idea being to start the year the way we want to end it: aware. Shortly after midnight, we have a silent "Zen party" with tea, hot cider, popcorn, and Chinese Chews.

4 eggs
1 cup sugar

2 cups dates, chopped
1 1/2 cups nuts, chopped
2 tsp. baking powder
1/2 tsp. salt
1 1/2 cups flour

1. Preheat oven to 350°. Sift dry ingredients together, adding dates and nuts once sifted.
2. In a separate bowl, beat eggs and add sugar.
3. Mix wet and dry.
4. Spread into a sprayed 10"x16" pan and bake for 30 to 40 minutes.
5. After baking, cut into small squares and drop each one in a paper bag with powdered sugar in it, shake, and set on a tray to cool.

Makes 50 cookies.

Chocolate Chip Cookies

These cookies don't last long around here. A rule of thumb that we go by: if you eat one or two, you just wanted a cookie; if you eat ten, something is going on that you may want to look into.

1/2 cup sugar
1/2 cup brown sugar
1 cup unsweetened applesauce
2 eggs or equivalent egg replacer
1 Tbs. vanilla
2 1/4 cups unbleached white flour
1 tsp. baking soda
1/2 tsp. salt

1 1/4 cups chocolate chips
1 cup toasted walnuts, chopped

1. Preheat oven to 350°.
2. Combine sugars, applesauce, eggs, and vanilla, mixing until well combined.
3. Combine flour, baking soda, and salt. Mix together wet and dry ingredients and add chocolate chips and walnuts.
4. Drop by spoonfuls onto cookie sheets sprayed with nonstick spray. Bake for twelve minutes, or until bottoms are browned.

Makes four dozen cookies.

Monks' Favorite Chocolate Cookies

3/4 cup applesauce

1/4 cup brown sugar, packed

1/4 cup sugar

1 egg or egg replacer

1 tsp. vanilla

1 tsp. peppermint extract

1 1/2 cups unbleached white flour

1/4 cup unsweetened cocoa

1 tsp. baking soda

1/4 tsp. salt

1 cup chocolate chips

1. Preheat oven to 350°. Mix applesauce and sugars in a bowl. Beat in egg or egg replacer. Stir in vanilla and peppermint extract.
2. Sift together the dry ingredients and add to the applesauce mixture along with the chocolate chips. Stir until well combined.
3. Drop by rounded teaspoonfuls onto cookie sheets that have been lightly sprayed with nonstick spray. Bake for ten minutes, or until bottoms are lightly browned.

Makes three dozen cookies.

Carmel Cookies

Invented, as you might expect, in Carmel, California, during one of our semi-annual retreats in that beautiful place.

1 1/2 cups wholewheat flour
2 1/2 cups rolled oats
1 Tbs. baking powder
1 tsp. baking soda

1/2 cup sugar
1/2 cup frozen apple juice
   concentrate
1/2 cup black coffee
2 tsp. vanilla

1 cup chocolate chips
1 cup walnuts

1. Preheat oven to 350°.
2. Mix sugar and wet ingredients together.
3. Mix dry ingredients together.
4. Add dry ingredients to wet, and mix well. Stir in chocolate chips and walnuts. (The dough will be rather thin.)
5. Drop by teaspoonfuls onto cookie sheets sprayed with nonstick spray, and bake for 12 to 14 minutes.

Makes three dozen cookies.

Ghirardelli Brownies

We like chocolate. This is our most requested dessert recipe.

2 eggs or egg replacers
1/2 cup sugar
1 tsp. Vanilla
1/2 cup applesauce
3/4 cup Ghirardelli Sweet Ground Chocolate and Cocoa[R]
2/3 cup unbleached, unsifted flour
1/4 tsp. baking powder
1/4 tsp. salt
1/4 cup chopped walnuts
1/4 cup chocolate chips

1. Preheat oven to 350°. Using a spoon, stir together eggs, applesauce, sugar, and vanilla.
2. Sift together cocoa, flour, baking powder, and salt. Stir into egg mixture. Add nuts and chocolate chips.
3. Spread into an 8x8-inch pan that has been sprayed with nonstick spray, and bake for 30 minutes.

Serves six to eight.

Chocolate Tofu Pudding
(from <u>Fat Free and Easy</u>)

1 10.5oz. package firm silken tofu
2 Tbs. cocoa
1/8 tsp. salt
1/3 cup maple syrup
1 tsp. vanilla

Place all ingredients into a blender or food processor and process until completely smooth. Chill before serving.

Serves four.

Rhubarb-Strawberry Pudding

6 cups rhubarb, cut into 1/2 inch pieces (approx. 1 1/2 pounds)
3/4 cup sugar
1/4 cup water
1 tsp. orange peel, grated
1/2 tsp. cinnamon

1 cup soymilk
2 Tbs. cornstarch
1 tsp. vanilla extract
1/2 tsp. almond extract

Graham crackers
1 cup strawberries (or many more), sliced

1. Combine the rhubarb, sugar, water, peel, and cinnamon in a pan and bring to a boil. Reduce to a simmer, and cook for about five minutes, or until the rhubarb is thoroughly mushy.
2. Dissolve the cornstarch in the soymilk. Add the extracts, stir, pour into the hot rhubarb mixture, and stir again.
3. As you bring the pudding back to a simmer it will thicken. Cook for one minute or so, then pour it into a serving dish and allow it to cool. Top with sliced strawberries.

This pudding is best served cold, but it's not bad warm either if you can't wait. Serve with graham cracker squares sticking out of the top.

Serves six to eight.

Graham Cracker Crusts

We have found several ways to make low-fat pie crusts. Here are a couple using graham crackers. Try them both and see which you like.

Version One:

1 package graham crackers (1/3 box)
2 Tbs. maple syrup or molasses
1 Tbs. applesauce or prune purée

1. Preheat oven to 350°.
2. Process the graham crackers in the food processor until they are fine crumbs. Add the remaining ingredients and pulse until well mixed.
3. Put into sprayed 8- or 9-inch pie pan and bake for eight minutes.

Version Two:

1 package graham crackers (1/3 box)
1 egg white, beaten

1. Preheat oven to 350°.
2. Process graham crackers until they are fine crumbs. Add egg white and cinnamon and pulse until well mixed.
3. Put into sprayed pie pan and bake for eight minutes.

Crumb Topping

2/3 cup wholewheat flour
1/2 cup rolled oats
2 Tbs. brown sugar
1/2 tsp. salt
1/2 tsp. baking soda

1/4 cup prune purée (preferably) or applesauce

1. Combine everything but the prune purée in a bowl.
2. Add the purée and mix together using your hands until all of the flour and oats are moistened. It is now ready to use.

This works well as a topping for a fruit pie or crisp and as a bottom crust. For a topping, sprinkle over the pie and bake for about twenty minutes at 350°. As a bottom crust, spread in a sprayed pie pan and bake at 350° for about 15 minutes, then allow to cool before filling. If the filling will need to be baked as well, then reduce the time above.

Apple-Berry Crisp

4 cups diced apples, peeled or unpeeled

1 cup water

3 packages frozen berries, any kind

1/4 cup sugar

1 Tbs. cinnamon

4 Tbs. cornstarch

1. Preheat an oven to 350°. Put the apples and 1/2 cup water in a pan and bring to a boil. Cover and steam until the apples are cooked, about ten minutes.
2. Add the berries (it's not necessary to defrost them first), sugar, and cinnamon and bring to a simmer.
3. Dissolve the cornstarch in the other 1/2 cup water, then pour this into the simmering fruit mixture and return to a simmer, stirring constantly.
4. When the mixture thickens, pour it into a sprayed 9x13-inch dish, cover with a double batch of Crumb Topping, and bake for 20 minutes, or until the topping is brown. Allow to cool for at least an hour before serving.

Serves eight to ten.

Tofu Chocolate Pie

As good, some have said, as the chocolate mousse you'll be served at a fancy restaurant. This recipe was the product of lengthy trial and error, much to everyone's delight.

1 9-inch pie crust, baked and cooled

1 1/2 10.5 oz. packs silken tofu
3 Tbs. cocoa
1/3 cup maple syrup
1 1/2 tsp. vanilla
1/4 tsp. salt

3/4 cup chocolate chips

1. Combine the tofu, cocoa, syrup, vanilla, and salt in a food processor until very smooth.
2. Melt the chocolate chips, add them to the mixture in the machine and again process until very smooth.
3. Pour into the pie crust and chill. The pie will firm up as it cools.

Makes one pie.

Lemon Meringue Pie

This pie may be the most fun thing to make in this whole book. It's a little tricky, but don't let that stop you. This can be a very beautiful dessert, especially if you ruffle the meringue with a spatula before you bake it so that drooping white peaks that have browned and set in the oven cover the finished pie.

1 pie crust

3/4 cup sugar

1/4 cup cornstarch

1 1/2 cups cold water

3 egg yolks, slightly beaten

grated peel of 1 lemon

1/3 cup lemon juice

1 Tbs. applesauce

3 egg whites

1/4 cup sugar

1. Preheat oven to 350°. In a medium saucepan, combine one cup sugar with cornstarch. Gradually stir in water until smooth.
2. Stir in egg yolks. Stirring constantly, bring to boil over medium heat. Boil one minute.
3. Remove from heat and stir in lemon peel, lemon juice and applesauce. Spoon hot filling into crust.
4. In a small bowl, beat egg whites until foamy. Gradually beat in 1/3 cup sugar until stiff peaks form. Spread meringue over hot filling, sealing to crust.
5. Bake at 350° for 15 to 20 minutes or until golden. Cool on rack and refrigerate.

Makes one pie.

Cherry Pie

4 cups fresh pitted cherries, or 2 packages frozen cherries
1/3 cup sugar
4 Tbs. cornstarch
1/2 cup lemon juice

1 tsp. lemon peel
1 1/2 tsp. almond extract
1/2 cup finely chopped almonds

1. Put the cherries in a pot and bring to a simmer. Cover and cook for ten minutes.
2. Combine the sugar and cornstarch in a small bowl and whisk in the lemon juice. Stir this into the hot cherries and cook over medium heat until thick (five minutes or less).
3. Remove from the heat and stir in the lemon rind and the almond extract.
4. Pour into a cooled pie crust and top with the chopped almonds. Allow the pie to cool for at least one hour before serving. It will set as it cools. Also good chilled.

Makes one pie.

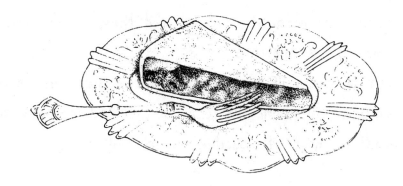

Pumpkin Pie

What would autumn be without pumpkin pie? We try to save a pumpkin from our garden until Thanksgiving to make this pie. It is possible to make it without eggs, if you prefer, by simply substituting two tablespoons of cornstarch for each egg.

1 pie crust

3/4 cup sugar
1/2 tsp. salt
1 tsp. cinnamon
1/2 tsp. ginger
1/4 tsp. cloves

2 eggs
2 cups cooked pumpkin
(see the How To section), or one 15-oz. can pumpkin
1 1/2 cups (1 12 fluid oz. can) evaporated milk (or soymilk)

1. Preheat oven to 350°. Combine sugar, salt, cinnamon, ginger, and cloves in a bowl.
2. Beat eggs in another bowl and then stir in the pumpkin and the sugar-spice mixture.
3. Stir in the milk and pour into the pie shell. Bake for 45 to 50 minutes, or until set. Can be served warm (allow to cool for at least an hour if possible) or chilled.

Makes one pie.

Chocolate Cake

One of our most popular desserts. You can use either the Chocolate Frosting on page 217 or the Tofu Chocolate Icing on page 218.

2 cups sugar

1 3/4 cups flour

3/4 cup unsweetened cocoa

1 1/2 tsp. baking soda

1 1/2 tsp. baking powder

1 tsp. salt

1 cup boiling water

2 eggs or egg substitute

1/2 cup soft tofu,
    blended in food processor

1/2 cup soymilk

1/2 cup applesauce

2 tsp. vanilla

DEEP DARK CHOCOLATE CAKE

1. Pre-heat oven to 350°. Coat with nonstick spray, then flour two 9-inch cake pans or a 9x13-inch rectangular pan.

2. Sift dry ingredients, then combine them in a large mixing bowl.

3. Add eggs, tofu, soymilk, applesauce, and vanilla. Beat on medium speed for 2 minutes.

4. Remove from mixer and stir in boiling water. (Batter will be thin.)

5. Pour into prepared pans and bake 30-35 minutes for round pans; 35-40 minutes for rectangular pan, or until a toothpick inserted in the center comes out clean. For round pans, cool cake for 10 minutes and remove from pans. Do not remove cake from rectangular pan.

Makes two 9-inch round cakes or one 9x13-inch rectangular cake.

A Glorious Child-Like Experience!

New Year's working meditation retreat at Carmel. The cook and I embark on the journey of creating the heavenly Chocolate Cake.

Multiply the recipe by five to feed the whole retreat group. Alas, I cannot remember how to multiply fractions! Feeling like I'm in grade five all over again. Luckily the cook remembers. Stirring, mixing, sifting, pouring into giant size bowls. Feeling like a midget in giant land. Fun, fun, fun to make Chocolate Cake!

Before we know it, it is time to pop the cake in the hot oven. Sore arm muscles, flour and chocolate on our clothes and in our hair. Total liberation to just get dirty and make chocolate cake! And then the best part of all. We get to lick the leftover batter off the wooden spoons, the spatulas and everything else with chocolate remnants. Yummy!

What a glorious child-like experience! Ahh, and then to eat Chocolate Cake in the sunlit courtyard for lunch. Does it get any better than this?

--from a retreatant (illustrations, too)

204

Carrot Cake
(from <u>The Peaceful Palate</u>)

A long-time favorite at the Monastery.

2 cups grated carrots
1 1/2 cups raisins
2 cups water

1/2 cup applesauce
1/2 cup maple syrup
1/3 cup sugar
1 1/2 tsp. cinnamon
1 1/2 tsp. allspice
1/2 tsp. cloves
1 1/2 tsp. salt

1 cup wholewheat flour
1 1/2 cups unbleached flour
1/4 cup protein powder
1 1/2 tsp. baking soda
3/4 cup chopped walnuts

1. Simmer grated carrots, raisins, and water in a saucepan for ten minutes.
2. Add applesauce, maple syrup, sugar, cinnamon, allspice, cloves and salt. Let stand until cool.
3. Preheat oven to 350°.
4. Stir together the flours, protein powder, baking soda, and walnuts. Add to the cooled carrots and stir just to moisten all ingredients.
5. Bake in a 9x9-inch pan coated with nonstick spray until a toothpick inserted into the center comes out clean (45 minutes to one hour).

Serves twelve or more

Raw Apple Cake

2 eggs or egg replacer equivalent

3/4 cup orange juice

1/2 cup applesauce

1 cup sugar

2 tsp. vanilla

1 1/2 cups whole wheat flour

1/2 cup unbleached flour

2 tsp. baking soda

2 tsp. cinnamon

dash salt

4 cups apples, diced

1 cup walnuts, chopped

1. Preheat oven to 350°. Combine eggs, applesauce, sugar, and vanilla.
2. Combine dry ingredients, and add dry to egg mixture. Add apples and walnuts.
3. Pour batter into a 9x13-inch pan that has been sprayed with nonstick spray, and bake for 30 to 40 minutes. Serve plain or frost with cream cheese frosting.

Serves ten.

Gingerbread

(from _The Peaceful Palate_)

This dessert becomes something special with Lemon Sauce (next page).

1/2 cup raisins

1/2 cup pitted dates

1 3/4 cups water

3/4 cup sugar

1/2 tsp. salt

2 tsp. cinnamon

1 tsp. ginger

3/4 tsp. nutmeg

1/4 tsp. cloves

2 cups flour

1 tsp. baking soda

1 tsp. baking powder

1. Preheat oven to 350°. Combine dried fruits, water, sugar, and spices in a large saucepan and bring to a boil. Continue boiling for two minutes, then remove from heat and cool.
2. Sift remaining dry ingredients, then mix thoroughly.
3. Mix wet ingredients, then mix wet and dry until just combined.
4. Spread into a 9 x 9 inch pan sprayed with nonstick spray and bake for 30 minutes, or until a toothpick inserted into the center comes out clean.

Serves eight.

Lemon Sauce

Wonderful with Gingerbread. You can make a lime sauce or an orange sauce with this recipe by substituting the juice and peel of limes or oranges in equal amounts.

1 cup water
1/4 cup sugar
1 Tbs. cornstarch

1/2 tsp. lemon peel
1 1/2 Tbs. lemon juice
pinch of salt

1. Combine sugar, cornstarch, and water in a double boiler.
2. Cook until slightly thickened.
3. Add remaining ingredients and serve warm or cold.

Serves four to six.

Walnut Crumb Cake

It's not easy to find a cake that works as well without the butter as it does with it. We found this recipe on the back of a flour bag, and it was an instant winner.

Streusel:
3/4 cup chopped walnuts or pecans
1/3 cup firmly packed brown sugar
1 tsp. cinnamon

Cake:
2 cups whole wheat flour
3/4 cup sugar
3 tsp. baking powder
1/2 tsp. salt

1 cup milk or soymilk
1/3 cup applesauce
1 egg

Glaze:
3/4 cup powdered sugar
1 to 2 Tbs. water

1. Preheat oven to 350°. Spray two nine-inch cake pans with nonstick spray.
2. Mix streusel ingredients until well blended and set aside.

3. Lightly spoon flour into measuring cup and level off. In a large bowl, combine flour and remaining cake ingredients until moistened.
4. Spread 3/4 cup batter into each pan and sprinkle 1/4 of streusel mixture evenly over batter in each pan. Carefully spread remaining batter over streusel in each pan. Sprinkle with the remaining streusel mixture.
5. Bake for 20 or 30 minutes or until toothpick inserted in the center comes out clean. Cool slightly.
6. In a small bowl, combine powdered sugar and enough water to make desired drizzling consistency. Blend until smooth. Drizzle over warm cakes.

Makes two cakes.

Chocolate Pudding Cake

1/2 cup unbleached white flour
1/2 cup whole wheat pastry flour
1/2 cup sugar
1/2 cup unsweetened cocoa
2 tsp. baking powder
1/2 cup soymilk
1/4 cup applesauce
1 tsp. vanilla extract
1/2 cup brown sugar, firmly packed
1 3/4 cups hot water

1. Preheat oven to 350°.
2. Combine the flours, sugar, baking powder, and half the cocoa in a bowl.
3. Combine the applesauce, soymilk, and vanilla in another bowl, and stir into the flour mixture. Pour the resulting batter into a sprayed 8" x 8" casserole dish.
4. Combine the brown sugar and remaining cocoa with the hot water and pour it over the cake. This may seem to you a very odd thing to do, but you'll see the purpose of it shortly.
5. Bake for 40 minutes. Remove from oven and cool in pan before serving.

Serves eight.

Italian Cheesecake

We appreciate dessert recipes that are low in sugar. This one is very elegant, especially with a little blueberry or strawberry sauce on top.

4 large eggs, separated
one graham cracker crust, or a couple handfuls of cookie or cake crumbs or ground almonds
2 pounds fat-free ricotta cheese
1/2 cup sugar
1/3 cup flour
1 1/2 tsp. vanilla
1/4 tsp. almond extract
1/4 tsp. salt
1 tsp. orange or lemon peel, or a combination
2 Tbs. lemon juice

1. Preheat oven to 375°.
2. Prepare a graham cracker crust (see page 196) in a large pie pan, or spray the pan with nonstick spray and cover with the crumbs or the ground almonds.
3. Beat the egg whites until they are stiff (see the How To section).
4. Beat together the cheese, egg yolks, and the remaining ingredients.
5. Fold in the egg whites (keep stirring to a minimum so that the egg whites do not lose their loft) and pour the mixture into the pan.
6. Bake for 45 to 55 minutes, or until the pie is solid in the center. Top with fresh fruit or berries, or Strawberry Sauce (next page).

Serves about eight.

Strawberry Sauce

You'll have to look hard to find anything more delightful than this sauce. We have a dedicated patch of strawberries in our garden that produces it for us multiple times in the spring. We'll have it on Cheesecake or Italian Cheesecake, or, for a special treat, we'll serve it with biscuits and milk for a Strawberry Shortcake.

1 cup fresh strawberries
2-4 Tbs. sugar
a few drops of lemon juice

1. Mash some or all of the strawberries in a bowl.
2. Add the sugar and lemon juice.
3. If you have saved out some of the berries, slice them and stir them in the berry and sugar mixture.

The same thing may be done with any berry, fresh or frozen. The amount of sugar required depends on the type of berry you use. If you prefer a smoother sauce, purée the whole thing in a blender.

Makes about a cup.

Tofu Cheesecake

Just as good as the dairy version--and even better, some say. If it seems impossible to you that a sweet made with tofu can be at all enjoyable to eat, try this one with the berry topping, or try the tofu chocolate pie. You will never think of tofu in the same way again.

1 graham cracker crust (see page 196)

1 pound tofu, drained
1/3 cup maple syrup
2 Tbs. lemon juice
1/2 tsp. salt
1 tsp. vanilla
2 Tbs. cornstarch

Topping:
1 cup fresh or frozen berries
1/2 cup plus 2 Tbs. apple juice
3 Tbs. maple syrup
1/8 tsp. salt
1 1/2 Tbs. cornstarch

For the cheesecake:
1. Preheat oven to 350°. Process the tofu in food processor until very smooth. Add remaining ingredients and process until well mixed.
2. Spread into the crust and bake for 30 minutes or until puffed and mostly set. It will set up considerably as it cools.

For the topping:

1. Combine berries, half-cup apple juice, syrup, and salt in a pot and bring to a boil.
2. Stir together cornstarch and remaining two tablespoons apple juice and stir this mixture into the fruit. Bring to a boil again and cook for one minute.
3. Pour over cooled cheesecake. Allow it to cool for a while, then chill for at least two hours, or overnight if possible.

Makes one cheesecake.

Cheesecake

This recipe makes a very good pie, a must in the spring when the strawberries are bountiful in the garden. We'll wait for a good harvest, and, when we get one, we'll mash half the berries and mix them with sugar. We pour this syrup over the cheesecake, slice the rest of the berries, and layer them on top. The finished product is as gorgeous to look at as it is wonderful to eat.

Filling:
16 oz. (2 packages) fat-free cream cheese.
1/3 cup sugar
4 eggs
1 1/2 tsp. vanilla extract
3 Tbs. lemon juice
1/2 tsp. grated lemon peel
1 pie crust

1. Preheat oven to 375°. Beat all filling ingredients together until smooth.
2. Pour into crust and bake for 25 minutes, or until set. Remove from oven and cool to room temperature.
3. Chill for at least two hours. Serve topped with sliced strawberries or peaches, Strawberry Sauce (page 213), or the berry topping that you will find with the Tofu Cheesecake (page 214).

Makes one Cheesecake.

Chocolate Frosting

This is the frosting we generally use on our chocolate cake.

1 1/2 oz. unsweetened chocolate
1/4 cup soymilk
1/3 cup sugar

1. Melt chocolate in a double boiler.
2. Put the milk and sugar in a blender and process on high speed until well combined.
3. While the blender is running, slowly dribble the melted chocolate into the milk/sugar mixture. Continue blending for one minute.
4. Remove from blender and refrigerate until ready to use.

Frosts one nine-inch cake.

Tofu Chocolate Icing

1 package silken tofu (see page 6)
1/4 tsp. salt
1 tsp. vanilla
1/4 cup cocoa
1/4 cup powdered sugar

1/2 cup chocolate chips

1. Process together all the ingredients except the chocolate chips until very smooth.
2. Melt the chips and add them to the tofu mixture, again processing until smooth. Chill. (The icing will stiffen as it cools.)

Frosts one large cake.

The Icing on the Cake

At the end of a workshop, a retreatant commented that he knew we were on to something the day we served chocolate cake. To his surprise, no one jumped or dove for it aggressively. There was no rush to get one's share. Rather, he noticed people took the time to enjoy their meal, and then some returned for a slice of chocolate cake, eating it slowly and mindfully. And there was plenty left over at the end of the meal! At the practice center where he used to reside, he said, it was customary that people dove for dessert as soon as it was set out on the table, and there was never ever any left over. What he witnessed in how dessert was treated here was an epiphany for him. It was proof that we were "on to something."

It's a funny compliment, but it points to a significant thing about this place. Deprivation is never supported. The belief that deprivation is a necessary part of spiritual practice is not encouraged. When we believe that depriving ourselves is necessary for spiritual growth, the whole day can be a struggle in which a piece of chocolate cake is the only sweetness we give ourselves. No wonder we would jump for a piece of cake if it was the only kindness we thought we deserved.

At the Monastery, the encouragement is to give ourselves lovingkindness, through subtle attention, in every moment. Lovingkindness as we rise, lovingkindness as we work, as we eat, as we go to sleep. This is not an easy thing to learn in the face of conditioning that says we deserve otherwise, but it is modeled in every part of how the Monastery works. We learn that kindness is an abundant resource, available in every moment. I project that all who come through feel the care that goes into everything, and that they learn how good it feels to receive care and to give care, and that everything and everyone deserves care. From this perspective, every moment of life is delicious, and dessert is just the "icing on the cake."

--from a monk

The Whole Shopping List Is About Me.

I am buying groceries. I still look upon myself as a monk. Job One for a monk is always to pay attention, to be awake. I tend to fall asleep when entering a grocery store, but usually I notice that I have checked out at some point and come back to the present. It goes like this:

I feel bad. I notice.

I believe others have better lives. I notice.

I envy their outfits. I smile.

I am jealous of their children's laughter. I comfort the mourning mother inside.

I first become sad, then aggressive at the sight of flesh in plastic wrap, barely resembling the pitiful remnants of a living being. I notice.

I feel guilty at having the choice of five different strawberry jams while others are starving. I notice.

I get angry at the aisles of liquors, available to anyone. I bow to the doctor inside.

Basically, I watch myself printing myself on any item in the store. This is fascinating. Like shopping my own Karma. The whole shopping list is about me. If it will start not being about me some day in this or the next lifetime, I will be home free. As long as this is not the case, my task is to watch all these projections arising and, ideally, let them pass away. But just noticing all these thoughts which very often are the causes of my suffering is much better than not being aware of them at all, even though I still have hours where I believe every word of this suffering reality to be completely true. I doubt myself all the time, but I never doubt practice. Life has become much easier this way.

Loaded with shopping bags, I make my way to the car. On the lot I pass two bicycles which have fallen on one side. I notice it and ignore it. I am already sitting in the car when I remember, "I am a monk!" I park the car again and put the bicycles back into a safe standing position. What a relief! Finally, I have started to take care of myself.

--from a former monk

Odds and Ends

It must be wonderful to be an odds and end, don't you think? There you are, so unique and special that they have to make a whole category just for you. It's too bad we could not put each recipe in its very own category; they all mean so much to us, each one in its own manner. In how many ways have all of us here suffered over our morning bowls of granola and fruit? In the silence, it feels as if everything in our environment witnesses our joy and our unhappiness as we follow each our own paths in this space. When you have struggled through one of those difficult days, where it seems impossible that you could ever see beyond your suffering again, what a great comfort it is to find yourself before a steaming bowl of spinach soup or a pile of blueberry pancakes. You have been through so much together already! The soup says, "It's going to be okay. I know you, and we have met in places other than this one. We are sure to find ourselves together again in some easier place before long."

So much has gone into these recipes, on so many levels, for so many years. Like each of us who practices here, and everyone who reads this book, each one has its place in the great scheme of things. The significance of it goes a lot farther than what we are going to have for supper--it is how we are going to live our lives. What will my plate of food teach me about who I really am? How might I learn about my own specialness from my bowl of kidney beans? In a way, everything is an odds and end. Isn't it fantastic?

Granola

Probably our most requested recipe. Granolas, generally, are made with oil and loaded with fat, but this is not necessary. This granola contains only the fat in the nuts and seeds.

12 cups rolled oats
3/4 cup millet
1 cup wheat bran
1/2 cup sunflower seeds
3/4 cup chopped almonds
1/2 cup sesame seeds

1 cup brown sugar
1/2 cup molasses
1 Tbs. vanilla
1/2 cup water

After Cooking:
1/2 cup flax seeds
3/4 cup raisins

1. Preheat oven to 350°.
2. Measure out all of the dry ingredients and mix them together.
3. Measure the wet ingredients into a small pot and heat it over a low flame until the brown sugar dissolves (it does not need to boil for this to happen). Stir often with a wooden spoon to prevent burning.
4. When the sugar dissolves, pour the wet mixture into the dry and stir together. It is important that the mixing happens right away to ensure that the liquid is evenly absorbed, and it is also good to stir from the bottom of the bowl so that everything is incorporated. Stir until well combined.

5. Spray two 9x13-inch "lasagna" pans with nonstick spray. Divide the mixture between them.

6. Place the pans side-by-side in the oven, and allow the granola to bake for 15 minutes. At the end of that time, remove one of the pans from the oven and stir it using a metal spatula. The granola will tend to brown more quickly (and eventually burn) where it is touching the metal pan, so the trick is to run the spatula along all of the surfaces and stir the browning oats into the rest of the granola. Return this pan to the oven and repeat this procedure with the other one. Open the oven door seldom during this process so that the temperature will remain constant and the granola will cook more evenly.

7. Bake for 10 more minutes and then stir again as before.

8. Bake once more for 10 minutes. Most likely the granola will be done at this time. Check to see that it has evenly turned a light brown color all the way through. If it appears as if some oats have not completely cooked (they would be pale in color next to the brown), then stir once more and bake for 5 more minutes. It's also good to check during this last 10 minute period in case the granola has gotten done early. The total cooking time will be 35-40 minutes.

9. Allow to cool for at least 15 minutes before adding the flax seeds and raisins. Pour the 2 pans of granola together into a bowl, sprinkle the flax seeds and raisins on top, and stir them in just enough to combine. The granola will stiffen and become brittle as it cools and will break up into little bits if it is stirred too much.

Prune Purée

We use this purée as a substitute for oil and butter when baking.

1 1/4 cups pitted prunes
boiling water

1. Plump the prunes by pouring the boiling water over them and allowing them to stand for 15 minutes, or more.
2. Purée the prunes in a food processor with 1/3 to 1/2 cup of water to make a smooth paste.

Makes about 1 1/2 cups.

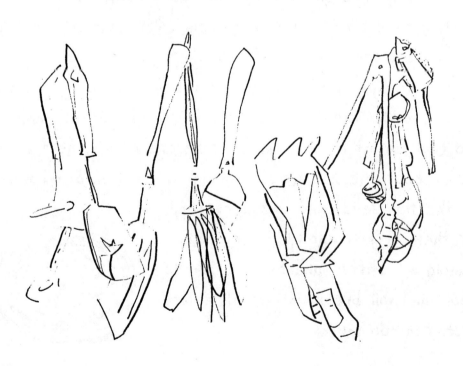

Soymilk

One of the most exciting things that has happened in our kitchen over the past couple of years has been the discovery of the possibility of making our own soymilk. Our soymilk has as much protein as cow's milk, is much lower in fat, and is very delicious. The following method is the product of a great deal of trial and error. In the early days there may have been some very challenging bowls of granola as a result, but as we played around with it, our soymilk became better and better. Now, it is very good indeed, most say. Soymilk is basically soybean tea. There are a couple of ways to go about it: the traditional method, making it as it has been made in China and Japan for centuries, and what is called the Cornell University Method. We began making soymilk in the old manner, and while it wasn't bad, there was a flavor in it that some people found very difficult to enjoy. We did some research and learned that this unpleasant taste is caused by an enzyme that is released into the milk when the beans are ground; the Cornell method was developed to prevent the release of this enzyme and to produce soymilk that more closely resembled cow's milk in flavor and so has more appeal to Westerners. We decided to try it, did a couple of experiments, and found the results so encouraging that we broke down and bought a fancy half-gallon steel blender to make our soymilk in. The difference in the milk that we made after that was remarkable, and even the monks who swore they would never have soymilk again, after the several disasters in the early days of our efforts, began to pour it over their morning oatmeal. Now we make it three gallons at a time and use over a gallon per day. It is as good for baking and in sauces and other types of dishes as it is with cereal, the cooks say.

The process is a little complex, but not difficult. Here is what you will need to make one gallon of soymilk:

Ingredients:
2 cups of dry organic soybeans
18 cups of water
a pinch of salt

Equipment:
- 2 large, thick-bottomed pots (able to hold 18 cups of water each)
- 1 colander, large enough to fit over the mouth of one of the pots
- a pressing sack (see below)
- a glass or steel blender

The pressing sack requires a word of explanation. You will need a piece of cloth that is big enough to fill the colander and drape over the sides when it is spread out; this piece of cloth will need to have been made with a relatively loose weave. You should be able to see through the tiny holes when you hold it up close. A bedsheet will be too tight; burlap will be too loose. Our current pressing sack is made from a number of thin hand towels that someone donated to us, sewn together. It is possible to buy a sack that is made expressly for this purpose. We know this because we have one that is too small, but we have been unable to find a source for a large one.

The method:
1. Wash the beans thoroughly, put them in a bowl and cover them with clean water, and allow them to soak overnight.
2. Put all 18 cups of water into one of the pots and bring it to a boil.

3. Set the colander in the mouth of the other pot and drape the pressing cloth inside. It should be wide enough to cover the entire lip of the colander and hang over the sides.

4. Wash the beans again, twice.

5. Here's the tricky part: you will need to grind the beans in the blender with the boiling water (this is why the blender needs to be made of glass or metal). It is the high temperature which prevents the release of the enzyme. Start with one cup of beans at a time. Put the beans in the blender, and at the same time as you turn the blender on, pour in enough of the boiling water that it fills the running blender without spilling over the sides. The water must be boiling; it will not work to have water that is merely hot. It's not a bad idea to preheat the blender before the first batch of beans to make sure the process happens at a high enough temperature.

6. Put the lid on the blender and grind the beans for one full minute.

7. Pour the resulting mixture into the cloth-lined colander, measure out another cup of beans, grind with boiling water as before, and so on until all the beans have gone through this process. You should have some water left in the pot--keep it boiling until needed.

8. Now you will press the milk from the ground soybeans (called "okara" at this point). Gather up all the corners and edges of your pressing cloth, twist them together, and gently press down. We like to use a potato masher or a glass jar for this because the milk is so hot. The liquid will be squeezed through the pores in the sack, leaving the okara behind.

9. When all the milk has been squeezed out, open up the sack once more, stir the okara, and then pour the remaining boiling water into the sack and press as before.

227

10. When you have extracted every drop of soymilk, remove the colander with the steaming okara and light a flame under the milk in the pot. It is necessary to cook the milk at a rolling boil to eliminate the raw bean taste that would otherwise be there. A light simmer is not enough; it must boil. You will need to stir frequently as the milk reheats so that it will not burn, and you will need to watch that it does not boil over. Just as the liquid comes to a boil it will foam up dramatically and attempt to spill out of the pot; if you are watching carefully you will catch it at that moment and lower the flame. You'll have to play with the heat until you get it just right (so that it boils without boiling over), and then after a couple of minutes of cooking the milk will no longer have the tendency to foam.

11. After 15 minutes remove the pot from the heat and allow it to cool. You'll want to refrigerate it as soon as you can; the sooner it cools the longer it will keep. We set it outside to cool in the winter.

At this point your soymilk is officially done. We like to add a pinch of salt to ours, and a little maple syrup (less than a half cup per gallon). You might, as an alternative, add honey or brown rice syrup, and you could have chocolate soymilk with the addition of cocoa. We like to keep some around without sweeteners in it to use in cooking. In the Orient, we're told, people rarely have their soymilk sweet; it's more common to find it served as a savory soup, which you could easily make with the addition of bouillon or other seasonings and perhaps some cooked onions and mushrooms. The leftover okara is a wonderful thing to add to breads and muffins or other baked goods, or to mix into pet foods.

Makes one gallon.

Soymilk Saga

Things are constantly in flux here at the Monastery. It's a good mirror of life. We humans like to pretend things don't change, but of course they do, constantly. Every moment, everything is different. After reading this sentence, you are different. I don't know that much about other Monasteries, or spiritual traditions, but I would guess experiencing change is a key part of any spiritual path. I heard a story of one Tibetan teacher who would teach his students chants, and just when they got them down and were feeling rather pleased with themselves and, let's face it, settled in their ways, he'd completely change the instructions.

What, you may be asking, does this have to do with food? Everything. What we eat is constantly being modified here based on, it seems to me, an ever-expanding awareness of, and movement toward, what is healthiest for body, mind and spirit. Case in point: Gradually our sugar consumption has drastically decreased, which is reflected in this new edition of our cookbook.

But the story I want to tell is of soymilk--how it was introduced to the Monastery, and how I resisted mightily. Because, just like Dr. Seuss's Sam-I-Am, I knew I did not like soymilk. And how, in the end, yes, just like Sam-I-Am and those green eggs and ham, I discovered I love the stuff. (How nice that the story has a happy ending.)

Before I lived at the Monastery, I had a friend who drank both milk and soymilk. She would ask her son, "Do you want cow's milk or soymilk?" This sounded very odd to me. Milk was milk. And I always drank milk. (The cow kind. The *real* kind.) Soymilk struck me as gross. Yuk. I wouldn't even try it.

When I moved to the Monastery we served cow's milk and we also had rice milk which we made. I decided to get up my courage and try it. I mean after all, I liked rice. And I'd made the rice milk, so I knew what was in it. So I tried it. I liked it!

Meanwhile, the Guide was looking at how to get more protein into our diets. "What about soymilk?" she asked. "I don't like soymilk. I like rice milk," a brave monk replied, which were my sentiments exactly, but I wasn't about to say anything. "Rice milk has no protein," the Guide responded. And just like that , we were serving soymilk instead of rice milk. "How did this happen?," I thought to myself. "I *hate* soymilk." I was very mad about rice milk being taken from us, and I resisted this soymilk intruder with a vengeance. ("With a vengeance" is an exaggeration, but I was definitely in the resistance camp, definitely NOT in the acceptance camp.)

Then we started making our own soymilk. And one day, as the soymilk maker, I decided to taste some of the freshly made brew. It was DELICIOUS! I couldn't believe my taste buds. Now, I love warm soymilk with tea--tea au soylait. And on the rare occasions I have coffee, I like it with soymilk.

Now, when it's just us monks here at the Monastery, all we serve is soymilk. We put cow's milk out only during retreats. I have to smile when I see all those retreatants pass the homemade soymilk on by and go straight for the cow's milk. If they only knew what they were missing.

Of course, it takes a lot of willingness to try something new, and to stick with it long enough to experience it and see what it's like without all our preconceived notions. You'd think soymilk would have taught me that lesson, that acceptance is way more pleasant a route than resistance. But here comes the Guide again with another one of her schemes, and I just know I'm gonna hate it. Choosing that all-too-familiar human response of resistance, I already DO hate it...or do I?

That's why we call it practice.

--from a monk

In the Beginning

The First Kitchen

The first kitchen was half of a 32 by 16 foot army tent. Within it was a giant propane refrigerator plumbed up to a ten-gallon propane tank that constantly needed changing. There was also a two-burner Coleman propane camp stove and a Coleman propane lamp. There was a homemade sideboard with the sink plumbed into a five-gallon bucket underneath. The water came into the sink from a tube attached to a five-gallon bucket above. This continually needed filling from the five-gallon water jugs lined up at attention outside the tent. When the five-gallon water jugs were empty, which was daily, we packed them into the back of our truck and drove one-half mile up the road where we filled them from the well of a very good neighbor. All in all it was quite adequate.

The food was stored in a very large wooden packing case. What it originally packed is long forgotten. The case, painted, stood up on end, which gave its lid a door effect. It stood right outside the back opening of the tent. It was called our "Pantry." The "Big" refrigerator, as it was called, even in the beginning when there was no small refrigerator, was crammed with perishables.

It was under these circumstances that I made my debut as a cook. Saying "yes" to being the cook took some very deep breaths and total willingness. Luckily, I didn't know too much. It's the best way to begin.

Where Is God?

Even in the early tent days we offered retreats. Our first retreat was a Meditation Retreat for about 25 people. By then, I had the knack of cooking in the semi-darkness of the tent on the two-burner propane camp stove. I had the two-pot meal down pat. However, cooking for 25 was a challenge under these circumstances. I remember being in the 100 degree tent, stirring a big pot of beans, when a retreatant poked her head in and whispered, "Where do you find God in this?" I remember looking up from my pot, sweat running down my brow, and whispering back, "God is all of this."

Hockey Puck Biscuits

The first kitchen tent was the scene of many delicious two-pot meals and was always alive with interesting aromas. However, as time went on, we all began to crave baked goods. As the Cook, I began to improvise. Finding a large cast iron pot, I began to "bake" on the camp stove. The results: hockey puck biscuits, black bottom corn bread, flat cake, and "fried" cookies. I guess we were desperate for bakery items because, as I remember it, we were all delighted with the attempts.

Expansion

Then there was the time we "improved" our living quarters by putting up a second 32 by 16 foot army tent next to the first tent. We created an L-shape with the two tents. The second tent became our meditation hall, which, up until this point, had been the other half of the first tent. Now we were able to expand. The first tent became half kitchen and half dining hall. Although the kitchen floor was a blue tarp, we felt very elegant because, on the dining side, the floor was a donated lime-green shag carpet. We considered this a great improvement.

The next wonderful thing was a new propane refrigerator to supplement the Big refrigerator. This one was much smaller and so was called the "Small" refrigerator. The day it came, it was properly installed. Our excitement dwindled to concern as we noticed the new, smaller refrigerator didn't seem to cool down below 70 degrees. We called the store, fearing we had received a defective appliance. We thought that, perhaps, all the jogs and bumps along the two-mile dirt road leading to the Monastery had knocked something off kilter. Being so new, it was still under warranty, so the store sent a repairman. He fixed and fiddled and pronounced it perfectly fine. He left. And we watched in dismay as the thermometer hovered around 70 degrees. Finally it dawned on us that this was the best this small refrigerator could do in an army tent where the temperature was 110 degrees. We let go of the idea of "refrigerator" and decided to use it as "a cooler" for a while--at least until winter.

The First Cookbook

Our Guide, Cheri, decided we needed to write a Retreat Cookbook, something like, "Fast and easy two-pot meals for retreats and ordinary time." We had no electricity, no computers, no typewriters. What we did have were pens, pencils, and binder paper. I huddled, night after night, next to the wood-burning stove in my hermitage, painstakingly handwriting out the first cookbook, with only a kerosene lamp to light the way. This handwritten cookbook, filled with all our favorite recipes, was used for years until it fell apart.

The First Real Stove

Later, we moved the whole kitchen tent to another location on the property. With that move we upgraded our cooking arrangement. We now had the use of a small apartment-size gas stove. This we plumbed to our ten-gallon propane tank. At our Monastery, at least when I was the cook, the cook also did all the plumbing and installation of the stoves and the sinks. This was a very good idea. That way when things broke down in the middle of meal preparation, which they mostly did, I could chop the carrots and fix the leak at the same time. We had come from a two-burner, two-pot-meal camp stove to a tiny (but real) gas range with four small burners and a small oven. The food had to take turns cooking, but we thought we were in Monastery heaven.

Weather Cooking

Some of the most memorable meals were cooked in the old kitchen tents. Mostly these were memorable to the Cook. These tents were all-weather tents-- open to all weather. It was interesting to cook in two shirts, a sweater, a thick jacket, a heavy vest, and two pairs of pants. Knit cap and gloves, two pairs of thick socks, and the required kitchen slippers completed the ensemble. All of us there at that time will attest that it was very hard even to move dressed like that, let alone cook. But cook we did, and great meals at that.

Summer cooking was a whole different story. 110 degrees is not conducive to cooking, or eating for that matter. It was conducive, however, to the creation of luscious uncooked cool meals, or almost cool, as the refrigerator never did cooperate in the summer. I know that those of us who lived there, or who attended retreats at the Monastery during this time, will fondly remember the salads and cold soups. All the old summer staples.

The New Kitchen

In March of 1995, the four or five of us living at the Monastery had the great experience of moving the entire inner workings of the kitchen and dining room into the nearly completed new building. What a sight to see the Big refrigerator and Small refrigerator, stove, and boxes being placed on a dolly and pulled and pushed up the path through the woods to their new home. Thus, we began a new era, a new chapter in the life of the Monastery. More training, more stories.

I give thanks for being the Monastery Cook and kitchen manager for so many years. I never did want to cook. I was willing. And the opportunities for training were endless. I have learned that "want to" does not necessarily have to play a part in what I do or do not do. After being the Monastery Cook, it seems as if all the "too's" in life have fallen away. Rarely is anything "too hard." I'm seldom "too hot, too cold, too late, too tired, too busy, too sick." There is just hot, cold, hard, busy, tired, sick. That makes such a big difference in my life. For all the training received, and all the training to come, I bow in deep gassho. I bow to the privileged environment, to the building, to the land, to all beings.

--from a former monk

234

The Fundamentals

I was one of only five monks in residence when I took over as the Cook. It was July, and I spent all those hot days that summer struggling to learn how to do my job, with, fortunately, only my four patient cohorts to track my progress. By the end of my career in the kitchen, two years later, I was feeding forty people at a time with a resting pulse rate--four would not even have been work--but I still feel very grateful for my gentle introduction. I had a great deal more to learn in those early days than how to make a casserole or how to cook a bean. I did not understand at all, at that time, how to take care of myself in the most fundamental way, and the silence and stillness in and all around the kitchen gave me the space to discover that for myself. Many times the other four monks would be working at a distance from the central part of the Monastery, and I would not even hear a noise created by another human being all day while I prepared their food. It's true that I worked as if I had a whole stadium full of people watching me with critical eyes, because that is how I had learned to survive, but it was hard not to notice in that solitude how unnecessary it was. The silence nourished me and pointed out the first steps on the way to compassion.

Then the summer ended, and we began to have more visitors. Every time somebody new arrived, I felt threatened, and I practiced trusting my own adequacy in the presence of more witnesses. I cooked for my first retreat in September, and if I did more than survive it at that time, I'd be surprised (I don't remember). But I know that I did survive and that my capacity to remain open in love to myself increased as the challenges of my job increased. It must have been in late October that I experienced my first really big retreat as the Cook. We had a get-together of folks in our Sangha from all over the country--there were going to be thirty of us--and it took all I had, as I remember, not to panic. Then I was informed of the schedule we would follow: group discussion three times a day (morning, afternoon, and evening), leaving only an hour in the morning after breakfast and a half-hour right before the evening meal to cook.

"It can't be done," I said. "This is impossible."

The Guide did not share my opinion. A few days later, I found myself in the kitchen with all my fellow monks and a few volunteers, with only an hour to fix a full spread for thirty people. Cheri was right, as usual. Everything got done, by a miracle, and turned out fine. And even more than that, I had a wonderful time.

Over the next few days I learned to love it: the kitchen jam-packed full of monks, chopping, measuring, stirring, slicing, washing and drying dishes, and everything else, every one of them completely devoted to the task in front of them (nobody can work like a monk can). I'm there directing all the action, enough energy in my body to run a washing machine. Nothing can stand up to that much focused attention; it was as if the food was cooking itself. I've found myself in this same situation countless times since then, and it always teaches me the same transforming lesson: that I am not alone on this earth, that it is not up to me to make life happen all on my own, that an abundance of support is available all around me for the asking.

It appears as if the days are over when only a handful of determined monks prowl around on this property. We are cooking for fourteen determined monks at every meal now, and our numbers are continuing to grow. I would have guessed that I would have missed those quieter days, but I don't. I feel like I get to have the best of everything. It's true that the sound of footsteps is almost always about these days, but I rarely overhear a human voice, and the experience of solitude is still intact. At the same time, I enjoy the support of the presence of the willing and dedicated people around me. I continue on my journey towards the discovery of my own adequacy to life, and so do they. It's an exciting adventure to be involved in.

--from a monk

For The Record

As I remember, I had been here for about three months when I got "the note." It said, "Please take over the duties of the Monastery Cook as of this morning. The Work Director will orient you after breakfast." This must be a mistake, I thought. Did I pick up somebody else's note? When I saw Cheri next, I tried to weasel my way out of it, but she was unyielding. "We all have to do what Life asks us to do," she said, and then, as sort of an aside, she added, "I don't make these decisions, you know." That's interesting, I thought, but who in the hell does? Now I understand what she meant, I think, which is that the whole thing, from beginning to end, is always just too perfect for a single intelligence to take credit for.

For the record, I hope it is clear that I had not asked for this job. More than that, I desperately did not want it, or any other job that involved anything like responsibility. All I ever wanted was to be left alone, and I had foolishly imagined that the Monastery would provide that opportunity for me. Responsibility terrified me--always had, as far as I could tell. Somewhere along the line I had picked up the idea that there was something wrong with me, and, until I came to the Monastery, my one ambition in life was to survive until I died without anybody else ever finding that out. I never did anything that would attract criticism if I could help it; I put my energy into staying invisible instead and accepted only the least threatening menial work I could find so that nobody would discover my incompetence. Imagine my horror then when I overheard one senior monk whisper to another on the morning of my promotion, "Does he know?" and the reality began to sink in that I had just been given the job I had avoided for all of those years, and, for the first time in my life, it would not be possible for me to hide.

I did the only thing I could do: I learned to cook. The process, though, was far from pretty. I couldn't quit, that was clear, and the panic that arose as I found myself in such an exposed and unprotected position, with the evidence of my inadequacy in front of people right there on their plates three times a day, sent me into a frenzy that lasted for months. Well, I would just have to be the best cook that anybody had ever seen. I would have to redo entirely the way the Monastery handled food (said my conditioning) so that it would all reflect me and

237

the image of competence that I needed to maintain. I would prove to them that I was not the bungler they thought I was, I told myself. The transition to cook happened in the middle of a big retreat, and the very first thing I did was to change the menu. I made a fried rice dish with an Indian peanut sauce, which wasn't all that bad for an amateur, as I recall, but it got me in all sorts of trouble. It was very gently pointed out to me that we do not cook with peanut butter here, and that, in fact, there are all sorts of guidelines about what we do and do not eat. I would be required to learn what they were and to follow them exactly. Oh, dear, I thought. This is not going well.

The next thing I remember is the infamous hot sauce episode. Soon after I took the reins in the kitchen, I was trained to go to town to do the shopping. It was explained to me that I was not to make any decisions while I was in the store. In particular, I was not to buy anything not on the regular shopping list unless specifically approved by the Guide. Okay, I can do that, I said. Well, a couple of months passed and I hadn't gotten in trouble in a while and I sort of forgot. Then one day while at the grocery store, I noticed they had this cool Vietnamese hot sauce with garlic in it, and it seemed like such a wonderful thing to have that I got some. Later I mentioned it to Cheri, sort of casually, and her reaction shocked me Her face got all red, her eyes bugged out, her veins bulged in her neck, and her teeth clenched. She said, "No! That is not okay. It is not okay to do that. You'll have to take it back." I was stunned. Nobody, since I was eight years old, had said such a thing to me.

Friends, I cannot describe the rage and the paranoia that followed. If ever in my life I have been capable of violence, this was the time. Looking back, I suppose that it felt as if the thing that I had been running from all that time had finally happened--that it had been seen that I was Bad--but all I knew then was that I was pissed and scared and I wanted out. It's a wonder I didn't split in the middle of the night. I hated Cheri and all the other monks, as well. I cooked their food with resentment, and I served it to them with a closed heart. I walked up to the main gate daily and gazed longingly down the road that led away from the Monastery, and on Sunday afternoons I walked for miles in search of some relief. For almost two months I struggled with all of this. Then one magical evening after the day's work was done, while walking on that road beyond the gate, I disidentified

238

and saw the suffering that had captivated me. In the relief of that experience I promised that, if it were in my power, it would never happen again.

It feels like it was at this point that I actually began spiritual practice because, of course, it did happen again, over and over. But now I had a hint of what was going on, and I enthusiastically (some of the time, anyway) went to work. Every morning my inadequacy would be waiting for me in the kitchen, and we'd spend the day wrestling for my body. In the beginning, as you might imagine, I lost most of the time. The urgency I suffered was intense. It was as if every meal was a test of my right to exist, and I worked in a frenzy to prepare for it. Failure was inevitable, and I would suffer the shame of it while the other monks were eating. But very slowly, as I was trained to watch the process as it happened, and as I learned to choose the breath over the fear, there began to be times when I did not suffer. Gradually I stopped running over the other monks in the kitchen.

After a while it became possible not to think about food every waking moment, and, bit by bit, I explored the possibility of happiness. My life, unfortunately, was a stream of miniature hot sauce episodes. I would be determinedly pursuing my egocentric agenda, deeply unconscious to the process that was driving me, and then I would crash into a roadblock set up by the Monastery, react in a fit of rage, and then, sooner or later, disidentify and see where I had been caught. The process was excruciating, and I lived in fear of the next impact, but it worked incredibly well. I recall one fiasco later in my cooking career that was especially grisly. We had a retreat coming up in Carmel--a very special occasion, with the likelihood of many of my favorite people being there--and I decided that the food would be the best the Monastery had ever produced. Everything was going to be new and impressive, and people would talk about how wonderful it was, and how wonderful I was, for days afterwards. I prepared for it for weeks, and if you overlook a couple of major disasters, the food wasn't at all bad, I suspect. But when we got back to the Monastery, I had a little meeting with the Work Director in which it was said, "Cheri was...surprised...by the Carmel menu." Oh, no. I was busted. I went back to my hermitage that evening in a desperate state and stayed up most of the night with the anger and humiliation that arose. In the morning, by a miracle, I let go, and it was never the same after that. It was still there--it is still here now--but it was never quite the same. Over and over again this sort of thing

239

happened, and through that process, what was not me was whittled away from what is Me. I began to actually live while I worked in the kitchen. I learned to relax and enjoy just cooking and to take care of myself when the urgency arose. I began to doubt my incompetence. Day after day I struggled with this, and day after day my experience improved. To my great astonishment (I feel it even now), a time eventually came when I felt like I was done. Not that the suffering was completely worn away, for I expect to work with it for the rest of my life, but I felt that the work that was there to do in the kitchen was finished. It was time for something else, and I was just screwing up my courage to ask for a demotion when another monk took over the cooking duties, and I was given an even worse job and started the whole process all over. That's the life of a monk, I suppose.

And now here I am, looking back in awe at the gift that Life gave me in all those experiences. Recently I have been aware of how significant it is for me that we are walking through the final steps in the production of this book because it is such an artifact of the training I endured in the kitchen all that time. And I am forced to admit that I've done the same process with this book as I did there. We began working on it ages ago, and had it not been for my resistance, I suspect it would have been published long before this. This is not the cookbook that I would have written. That is to say, this is not the cookbook that "I"--the illusion of a separate self that I was taught to believe is me; the parasite that lives on my life force and intelligence; the cruel standard bearer that is devoted to my suffering--would have written. The cookbook that I would have written would have been full of fat and very fancy and inaccessible to as many people as possible. This book, in contrast, is a product of compassion. It is a representation of the miracle of the teachings and of the sincerity of everyone who has ever chopped an onion or baked a cookie in our kitchen. It is an expression of the possibility of life beyond suffering because it is the result of the practice that leads me and so many others in the direction of freedom. Every aspect of its creation has been a teaching for me, for which I cannot even begin to express my gratitude.

The work of many people has gone into this book, from the cooks who have prepared our food, to the many generous souls who have given us the means to provide it for ourselves, to those that have enjoyed it and taken the memory of it home with them into their lives. The parts of it that are a product of my own training, I freely offer in lovingkindness to anyone who may benefit from them, and I wish you all the same good fortune with these recipes that I have had.

--from a monk

*Rhea is a little four-legged friend who lives at the Monastery.

The following sits at the end of our serving table:

Mindful Eating

Eating is a concrete way of expressing compassion for oneself. The life force is in the food. The life force is in the breath. Together they create and sustain us. To express gratitude for it all, we can be present, mindful, compassionate, and accepting with each bite. Chewing in grateful acceptance, breathing while chewing, putting down utensils between bites, and making Gasshō with each bite, are some ways of expressing gratitude for the food that sustains us, and the body that we dwell in.

References

Here is a list of our favorite cookbooks. We feel indebted to the authors for all the help and encouragement their work has provided, and we wish for you to have the same experience. We highly recommend these books. We hope you will be inspired, by what you find in our cookbook, to branch out and explore the many possibilities offered herein and elsewhere.

Raymond, Jennifer. _Fat-Free & Easy: Great Meals in Minutes_. Book Pub Co; (February 1997)

----. _The Peaceful Palate_. Book Pub Co; Revised edition (August 1996)
If there were such a thing as our favorite cookbook, this would be it. We have probably made every recipe in it. Our copy fell to pieces years ago, and we had to put it in a binder. The pages are covered with notes about quantities and cooking times in a dozen handwritings, and stained by years of spills and drips. We had the honor to talk with Jennifer Raymond in person as we sought permission to use her recipes, and she told us that we were more than welcome to them. She wants, more than anything else, to spread the idea of non-violent cooking to as many people as possible. A woman after our own hearts, to be sure. And, as if that weren't enough, she sent us a new copy of the book, complete with the cover that many of us had never even seen, it was lost so long ago. If you have room on your shelf, beside our cookbook, for only one more, this would be the one.

Clarke, Christina. _Cook with Tofu_. Avon; (June 1986)
Dave discovered this book at the home of a friend when he was out visiting one time. He was so impressed by what he found that he photocopied the whole thing and brought it back to the Monastery with him. If this book is still in print, you will be glad to have it, as it is full of wonderful ideas about cooking with tofu, from salads to main dishes to desserts.

Gregory, Patricia R. _Bean Banquets_. Santa Barbara, CA: Woodbridge Press, 1984. This book contains bean dishes from all over the world. Everything we've tried we've liked. Several of our favorite curried dishes were inspired by this book.

Hinman, Bobbie. _The Meatless Gourmet: Favorite Recipes from Around the World._ Roseville, CA: Prima Publications. Spiral edition (October 1994).
This book has been one of the pillars of the Monastery kitchen for many years. The author apparently traveled all over the world, adapting the food she found to a meatless diet and published it in this excellent book.

Johnson, Ellen Foscue. _Garden Way Publishing's Original Bread Book._ Garden Way Publishing, 1979, now published by Storey Communications of Pownal, VT.
This book was given to us by our wonderful neighbor, Joan Thurlby. Many of our favorite muffin recipes and several of our yeasted bread ideas came from this book.

Katzen, Molly. _The Enchanted Broccoli Forest._ Berkeley: Ten Speed Press, 1995.
----. _Moosewood Cookbook._ Berkeley, Ten Speed Press, Revised edition, 1992.
----. _Still Life with Menu._ Berkeley: Ten Speed Press, Revised edition 1994.
Anyone familiar with these books knows Molly Katzen for the incredibly gifted cook that she is. _Moosewood_ is one of the most successful cookbooks of all time, and for good reason.

Raichlen, Steven. _High-Flavor Low-Fat Vegetarian Cooking._ Penguin USA (Paper); Reprint edition (May 1997).
This book is a relatively new find for us, and much of it is unexplored, as yet, but the possibilities are very exciting. This is a good one for people who would like to play around with things that are a little fancier. It is a beautiful book to read, and the dishes are elegant.

Robertson, Laurel, Carol Flinders and Bronwen Godfrey. _Laurel's Kitchen._ Ten Speed Press; (November 1997).
This one is a classic. It has been helpful to us in all sorts of ways over the years, and we are indebted to it for many of our favorite dishes. It also contains nutritional information, some of which is outdated now, but much of which is still very useful.

Schlesinger, Sarah. _500 Fat-Free Recipes._ _A Complete Guide to Reducing the Fat in Your Diet._ New York: Villard Books, 1994.
This one is filled with simple recipes and good basic cooking information. It is perfect for people new to cooking for themselves.

Shurtleff, William and Akiko Aoyagi. _The Book of Tofu._ New York: Ballantine Books, 1992.
Here is a wonderful book about a wonderful food. If you are interested in making your own tofu (as we are), this would be a good resource for you; much of what we learned about making soymilk came from this book. It also contains many traditional Japanese tofu recipes, and we have had good luck with the ones we've tried.

This is an extremely fortunate time to be a vegetarian. The variety of foods available is amazing, and the many outstanding cooks and cookbooks you run across will continually inspire you to explore who you are through the food you eat. We would love to support you in this exploration, so if there is any way we can be of assistance, let us know.

Books from Cheri Huber

Published by Keep It Simple Books & Zen Meditation Center
All titles are available from your local bookstore.
To order, call 800-337-3040. Fax orders: 209-728-0861.
To order by mail, use this form or a separate sheet of paper
and send order and payment to the address below.
Visa, Mastercard, and Discover accepted.

____	There Is Nothing Wrong With You*	0-9636255-0-0	$12.00
____	There Is Nothing Wrong With You for Teens	0-9636255-1-X	$12.00
____	How You Do Anything Is How You Do Everything: A Workbook	0-9636255-5-1	$10.00
____	The Depression Book*	0-9636255-6-X	$12.00
____	The Fear Book*	0-9636255-1-9	$10.00
____	Be the Person You Want to Find*	0-9636255-2-7	$12.00
____	The Key and the Name of the Key Is Willingness*	0-9636255-4-3	$10.00
____	Nothing Happens Next	0-9636255-3-5	$8.00
____	Sex and Money: A Guided Journal	0-9636255-7-9	$12.00
____	Suffering Is Optional	0-9636255-8-6	$12.00
____	That Which You Are Seeking Is Causing You To Seek*	0-9614754-6-3	$10.00
____	Time-Out for Parents*	0-9614754-4-7	$12.00
____	The Monastery Cookbook	0-9614754-7-1	$16.00
____	When You're Falling, Dive	0-9710309-1-X	$12.00

*Also available as a book on tape. Call for prices.
Books and tapes are sold in discounted sets. Call for prices and a catalog.

Name: _____

Address _____

City: _____ State _____ Zip _____

Please send the books I have checked above $ _____

Postage and Handling** $ _____

7.25% Sales Tax (California residents only) $ _____

                        TOTAL ENCLOSED $ _____

**Add $3.00 shipping for each book. Overpayments will be refunded.

If ordering by mail and using a credit card, send name, address, card number and expiration date to:
KEEP IT SIMPLE, P.O. BOX 1979, MURPHYS, CA 95247

Orders out of U.S. send double postage.
A complete catalog will be sent with your order.
Wholesale inquiries call 209-728-0420

There Is Nothing Wrong With You
An Extraordinary Eight-Day Retreat
based on the book
There Is Nothing Wrong With You: Going Beyond Self-Hate
by Cheri Huber

Inside each of us is a "persistent voice of discontent." It is constantly critical of life, the world, and almost everything we say and do. As children, in order to survive, we learned to listen to this voice and believe what it says.

This retreat, held at the beautiful Zen Monastery Practice Center near Murphys, California, in the western foothills of the Sierra Nevada, is eight days of looking directly at how we have been rejecting and punishing ourselves and discovering how to let that go. Through a variety of exercises and periods of group processing, participants will gain a clearer perspective on how they live their lives and on how to find compassion for themselves and others.

This work is challenging, joyous, fulfilling, scary, courageous, demanding, freeing, loving, kind, and compassionate—compassionate toward yourself and everyone you will ever know.

For information on attending, contact:
Zen Monastery Practice Center
P.O. Box 1979
Murphys, CA 95247
Ph.: 209-728-0860
Fax: 209-728-0861
Email: information@thezencenter.org

E-MAIL CLASSES
with
Cheri Huber

Cheri Huber conducts interactive e-mail classes.
To be notified of future classes,
send your name, e-mail address, and phone number to zen@mlode.com
or visit www.thezencenter.org
or www.cherihuber.com
These classes are offered by donation.

For a schedule of workshops and retreats, contact us in one of the following ways:

Website: www.thezencenter.org

Email: information@thezencenter.org

Zen Monastery Practice Center
P.O. Box 1979
Murphys, CA 95247

Telephone: 209-728-0860

Fax: 209-728-0861

For a one-year subscription to the Center's quarterly newsletter and calendar of events,
In Our Practice, send a check for $12.00 along with your name and address.